Martin Winiecki (Ed.)

SETTING FOUNDATIONS
FOR A NEW CIVILIZATION

Perspectives for the Global Revolution
Study Materials from the Terra Nova School

I0103498

About the book:
This book contains the latest contributions from the Tamera Peace Research Center in Portugal. At a time when the media is full of reports on war and catastrophes, a mental-spiritual gateway to another option for development is opening up: Our planet, with its people and animals, its landscapes and bodies of water, is curable, if we want and manifest this healing with all our might.

The individual articles are study texts for the Terra Nova School. Groups of people throughout the world have begun studying these ideas and disseminating them within their networks and circles of friends. They are working together to build global awareness of the fact that such a profound systemic change can succeed and how it can be done. It is a new kind of revolution that is without precedent. A new human impulse, non-dogmatic and open to all who wish to join, is now inconspicuously paving its way.

ISBN 978-3-927266-47-6

© 2013, Verlag Meiga, 1st Edition

Original title: *Grundsteine legen für eine neue Zivilisation*

Layout: Juliane Paul

Translation: Barbara Pavlik, Cameron Phelps, Douglas Baillie, Joshua Gottdenker, Jens Burkhardt, Jeff Anderson, Rabea Herzog, Sten Linnander, Dara Silverman

Cover: (CC) by openwalls.com

Printed by Lightning Source Ltd. UK/USA

What goal would awaken humanity's enthusiasm?

What vision would inspire humanity to fight for its survival and the survival of the whole planet?

For what goal would humanity leave behind all quarrels to manifest it with united powers?

CONTENT

Foreword by the Editor   7

I THEORY OF GLOBAL HEALING

Terra Nova
Project for a Free Earth   15
Dieter Duhm

Global Campus
A Declaration of the Basic Thoughts and Goals   21
Dieter Duhm

The Earth Needs New Information   40
Monika Alleweldt

II THE HEALING OF LOVE

Community as a Research Subject
Excerpt from: Project Declaration I   61
Dieter Duhm

There Will Be No Peace on Earth as Long as There is
War in Love

Manifesto for the Founding of the   63
Global Love School
Sabine Lichtenfels

The Importance of a Global Love School   65
Free Speech for the Opening of the Global Love School
Sabine Lichtenfels

The Healing of Love
Why the Issue of the Love Between the Genders   78
had to Become the Central Focus of Our Project
Dieter Duhm

III THE MATERIAL BASIS

The Secret of Water as a Basis for the New Earth
Healing the Water Cycle through the Creation of
Water Retention Landscapes
Bernd Walter Mueller   91

Peace with Nature and All Fellow Creatures
Excerpt from the Book: The Sacred Matrix
Dieter Duhm   108

IV APPENDIX

Biographies of the Authors   114
Donations   118
Literature   119

TERRA NOVA SCHOOL.
NETWORK FOR A GLOBAL SYSTEM CHANGE

Foreword by the Editor

This book contains study texts for the Terra Nova School, a global education network initiated in May 2013. The Terra Nova School is to become a catalyst for a global system change. Its aim is to empower and unite those who wish to work toward a new Earth that is free of violence and war.

Within the first few weeks we have received many applications as well as positive feedback from all over the world. The first study groups are now being formed in over thirty countries in Europe and the Middle East, North and South America, Africa, Asia and Australia. We are working together on a perspective for the healing of humankind and the earth. We want to give a humane direction to the global revolution in which we live. We invite you to participate!

In this book, we offer insights into some key areas of peace education, with basic texts by the school's senior teachers, Dr. Dieter Duhm, Sabine Lichtenfels and Bernd W. Müller. We start with the theoretical foundations of the new peace centers and models for the future, which are summarized in the global "Healing Biotopes Plan." This plan shows why and how a new peace development on our planet could prevail within a relatively short period of time in spite of the apparent supremacy of systems of violence. Following are the texts from the founding of Tamera's Global Love School where we examine the core human issues of community, sexuality, love and partnership. This book concludes with two essential aspects of the ecological structure of the new culture: the concept of Water Retention Landscapes and non-violent cooperation with animals and all creatures.

The Terra Nova School consists of local groups that study this information and share it with friends, neighbors and other interested people, as well as with networks and movements. These are learning circles and "revolutionary cells" that meet weekly to work through and deepen the issues together. At the beginning of each month they receive a training package with study texts, speeches, videos and recommendations for further reading on the current core areas. Monthly offerings include live-stream online seminars and speeches from Tamera. In addition, the local groups organize political gatherings, readings, film screenings and art activities in the different cities and countries to bring new ideas to the public. They celebrate action days, such as the annual Global Grace Day on November 9th, and come together once a year for a common meeting of the global learning community. The individual participants and groups are no longer working alone, but rather are seeing themselves more and more as part of a new planetary community.

The Terra Nova School originated in the Tamera Peace Research Center in southern Portugal. Tamera researches fundamental aspects of a post-capitalist society and implements them, as far as possible, in the form of a model. The project, which was originally founded in Germany by Dieter Duhm, Sabine Lichtenfels and others, is based on 35 years of inter-disciplinary research. Social, spiritual, ecological, and technological studies are coming together here in a way of life that is being put into practice. About 200 co-workers and international students are presently involved in the development of the project.

As part of the young generation in Tamera, we are establishing the Terra Nova School as a worldwide cooperative for all who wish to join this work. It is our response to the unspeakable suffering that occurs every day on our planet.

The global revolution, which is flaring up in more and more places, marks the collapse of existing societies. The protests, from the Arab Spring to Istanbul and Brazil, are no longer the struggles of certain political ideologies; they are the fundamental human cry, "Enough! An end to this madness!" We are hearing the outcry all over the world.

The era of imperialism is over. The old system finds itself irretrievably in collapse – socially, ecologically and economically. A new development has begun on Earth. New life forces are rising up against the walls of a millennia-old era of violence and seeking a new world. Despite all the opposition, the forces of life cannot be stopped in the long run. Now we need a common vision in order to develop a power of peace that is stronger than all violence.

For this, the movement needs places to develop and demonstrate the new perspective. This starts with the dissemination of thoughts and ideas through promoting the corresponding books and papers and by organizing events. Interested people will join together to form study groups which give rise to communities over time. The groups operate specialized bookstores, cafes and cultural centers, farms with Water Retention Landscapes, and even model universities and whole Healing Biotopes. These are the heralds of the coming peace society. The people who work for Terra Nova follow, with increasing dedication, certain ethical guidelines such as truth, mutual support and responsible participation in the whole. These are basic principles for a humane culture. They apply to ecological and social fields as well as the most intimate questions of sexuality, love and partnership. Thus the inner focus of each individual is changed from a matrix of fear and separation to a matrix of trust and cooperation. Through inner twists and turns and the corresponding external actions, the participants of the planetary movement will regain the positive power to act, which they have previously succumbed to society and state. The new revolutionaries are no longer working in reaction to a collapsing system, but with a view to the new reality that they are giving birth to through their minds, spirits, hearts and hands. The system change is already under way, if we cooperate with each other properly.

We can perhaps compare the transition to the new era with the transformation of a caterpillar into a butterfly. An entirely new organism is formed from the material of the old one. Just as the butterfly is already living in the caterpillar as an inherent higher self so lives Terra Nova, the new Earth, as the hidden potential already existing in this world and within us. Life has a tremendous capacity for self-healing. This capacity is within every living organism, even those that are very badly injured. The more we see this healing potential and can apply it to our own thoughts and actions, instead of focusing on momentary defects and injuries, the more effective the healing powers can be and ultimately bring about the tipping point. The following task goes to the peace forces of the Earth – Find the thoughts, words and images that activate the manifestation of a newly healed world! The Terra Nova School puts itself in service of this work. We are looking forward to our future cooperation.

In the name of love for all that lives.

Martin Winiecki
Tamera, Portugal, July 2013

I THEORY OF GLOBAL HEALING

TERRA NOVA

Project for a Free Earth

Dieter Duhm, 2013

Our current society is collapsing because of inner contradictions, which can no longer be solved by conventional means. The human being is a "Zoon Politikon," a societal being, and as such is subject to the laws of society. At the same time however, in accordance with his physical and spiritual nature, he is a member of the biosphere and is thereby subject to the laws of organic life. If these two laws contradict each other, disease, criminality, violence and war arise. Today we experience a planetary culmination of this contradiction. We experience global epidemics of disease and violence. Humankind has organized itself in the wrong way. It has established a way of living that does not comply with the laws of life. We have reached an apocalyptic limit beyond which no survival is possible.

To overcome this dead-end we do not need megacities nor trillion dollar technologies for Martian colonization. Instead we need intelligent concepts for a new cohabitation of planet Earth. We do not need reform, instead, we need a new direction of human evolution. We are at the beginning of the greatest revolution in history.

The new way requires reintegrating human life into the basic laws of the universe and the Earth. These include ethical, social and "biotopical" laws. Any violence we inflict upon our co-creatures will come back to us as disease or insanity. The coming civilization is devoid of any cruelty. Plants and animals are cooperation partners in the evolution of our biosphere that we experience together.

In the Tamera project we have been working toward putting these thoughts into practice for eighteen years. In new ecological, technological and social research areas, we are trying to integrate our human world into the higher world of life. Above all, we are working on retention landscapes for the healing of water and on new social systems for the healing of love. Millions of children are helpless and lost because their parents are in broken relationships. Infinitely many human tragedies are caused by unfulfilled longings and failed love relationships. To end the secret war between the genders we need a new social and ethical order and a new vision of love. For the healing of love, as for the healing of water, the existing forms used to imprison life need to be overcome and replaced by organic forms. The ecology of the new era consists of a non-violent cooperation with nature and all its beings. The technology of the new epoch is no longer based on breaking resistance, explosion, but is based on resonance with the powers of nature. Water shows an incredible power of self-purification when we allow it to flow naturally, instead of forcing it into artificial channels. Nature works with incomperable technologies in all areas. It contains inherent healing powers with which it can survive and heal even the strongest devastations. This applies to the healing of the human body as well as to the healing of the entire biosphere. The inner life force of nature showed itself in our project in southern Portugal where we were able to transform an eroded and almost desiccated landscape through building water retention areas into a paradise of plants and animals. Still today, such local healing possibilities are blocked by the practices of globalization, often through the use of military force. Today we experience a global war between the powers of life and the forces of destruction. The powers of life will succeed if peace workers from all around the world see a realistic utopia and if the world's indignation is connected with the great conception of the new Earth. If life wins there cannot be any losers.

Famines and natural disasters are almost always the consequence of human mismanagement caused by the politics of banks, secret societies and corporations. Their time however, has passed. The epoch of capitalist globalization cannot be continued without unimaginable bloodshed and without the destruction of nature on a massive scale, a fact which banks and corporations know full well. Their Illuminati should consider if they will change sides soon enough. The global search for an alternative now has to include the laws of life and it needs to acknowledge that animals, even those that are bred for slaughter or fur, have a heart and soul. Here lies the deepest system change: the change from a murderous mechanism to a system of compassionate aid, not only in the sense of the Christian ethics of 'love thy neighbor,' but in the sense of the cosmic order, which we call the "Sacred Matrix."

Water, food and energy are freely available to all human beings if they are produced according to the laws of nature and not the laws of profit. The almost infinite productive powers of nature enable almost infinite possibilities of self-sufficiency. The system change from the law of profit to the law of life is not a question of ideology but a question of collective survival.

All of life and all communities of natural life are organized according to the pattern of the Sacred Matrix. All beings are connected through an inner matrix, which expresses itself in human relationships as trust, solidarity and mutual support. Those inner qualities also apply to human beings and all of nature's co-creatures. Terra Nova, the image of the new Earth, shows a human civilization that has a relationship of trust and solidarity with the civilizations of the natural kingdoms that surround it.

The human world needs new information. For thousands of years it has been steered by the information of violence and war. Nations have persecuted and slaughtered each other. All current states originated from a history of bloodshed. The pains that were suffered there are cruel beyond description. They were passed on from century to century. This diabolical chain has left vile wounds in the collective body of humanity. We all suffer from a global trauma that has left dark images and fears in our collective soul. The trauma will be passed from generation to generation until we have understood its causes and removed them. Many attempts at renewal, many appeals for peace, many alternative projects fail due to the collective wall that has formed over the course of thousands of years of war inside the human being. It is the wall of the closed heart. The task of the new centers consists of overcoming this historic trauma, of opening this traumatic wall ("body armor") and of changing the hologram of fear into a hologram of trust. In order for this to succeed we need to flip a global switch. The switch that has so far activated the information of violence and war has to be turned now to the information of trust and cooperation. This happens not only through prayers but through concrete planning and manifestation of the new world. We have to decide on which side we stand. In our houses and gardens, in our facilities for water, energy and food, in our love relationships and partnerships, and in our social and political systems, we decide which information is sent to the world. The implementation of the new centers is a collective decision of human beings who are conscious of the situation and who therefore turn their inner switch in the direction of life: the direction of solidarity and cooperation, trust and truth – even truth in love. How much violence and suffering has been triggered just because of lies in love! There cannot be peace on Earth as long as there is war in love. Nowhere is the traumatic damage as strong as in the areas of love and community. Through the loss of community, humanity has lost its ethical source. To recover our original values such as truth, solidarity and trust we need functioning communities. Building functioning communities of trust is one of the highest and most difficult goals of the current revolution.

The new civilization is emerging out of a network of new centers which are all connected with the laws of the universal order of life. In this connectedness the carrier wave of "morphogenetic field building" is at work. Because they are all relating to the same order, the Sacred Matrix, they retrieve the same information from the cosmic database, which is necessary for realizing the epochal steps. As soon as the mental/ spiritual carrier field is set, the morphogenetic field process begins by itself. A new global field is forming. It spreads underground as if like the mycelium of a fungus and brings forth new forces with the power to break through concrete slabs. The result of this new historical process is easy to see... All over the world new cells arise – the gardens and retention landscapes, the schools and libraries, the model universities and Healing Biotopes, which spread the message of a new life. Humanity has ripened for this shift. The Arab Spring has become a global revolution that has found its great, humane goal. Here reigns no violence, but the solidarity of a new planetary community.

We are working internationally on building global Healing Biotopes. The "Global Campus" is an international university with campuses in different countries where the basic thoughts and goals of our work shall be taught and manifested. In the center of the present work stands the peace school Tamera in southern Portugal. We need sponsorship to continue our work. Here's to a joyful and productive cooperation!

In the name of affection for all creatures.
In the name of all children.
In the name of love.
Thank you and Amen.

GLOBAL CAMPUS
A Declaration of the Basic Thoughts and Goals

Dieter Duhm, 2012

What is the Global Campus?

The Global Campus is a worldwide education platform for a future without war and for the development of appropriate models. The base camp for the Global Campus is Tamera Peace Research Center in Portugal. Those involved are people and projects which have decided to collaborate on a global level. They see the need for global peace models and are committed to realizing them. The development of peace models under various regional conditions is taught and researched. Participants of the Global Campus affirm the basic ideas and goals that are described in the following sections.

The Global Campus is developing a network of autonomous centers that follow a common ethical, social and environmental code. At the core of the global healing work is a new alliance of human beings with all co-creatures. For peace to be achieved on the outside, it is crucial that it arises on the inside amongst human beings. The project orientates itself both in theory and practice along the following guidelines:

- Realignment of the human world with the higher-world order of life and creation
- Non-violent cooperation with all co-creatures. No violence against animals – not even against animals such as rats and snakes
- Healing of water through the development of "Water Retention Landscapes"
- Development of permaculture and self-sufficient food supply

- Withdrawal from the oil industry and the development of autonomous energy systems
- Establishing decentralized subsistence economies
- Establishing functioning communities
- Following ethics of truth, mutual support and responsible participation
- Ending the war between the genders and all sexual humiliation
- Truth in love and no deceit in partnerships
- No revenge – Grace instead of retribution

These are guidelines for the coming world society with its new universities and new ways of living. With them a new planetary order will come into existence in which all creatures of our planet will be connected with each other, because this order is in accordance with the world order, which we call the "Sacred Matrix."

During their international pilgrimages between 2004 and 2008, Sabine Lichtenfels and Benjamin von Mendelssohn developed the idea of a world university in the form of the Global Campus. The guiding idea was Grace – to change the pattern of anger and hatred into a pattern of human compassion and solidarity. The pilgrimages took place in Israel-Palestine, Colombia and Portugal. Sabine Lichtenfels writes,

"I was guided by the question of how a future without war can be achieved. I described the ethics and philosophy of the Global Campus in my book 'Grace – Pilgrimage for a Future Without War.' While the students learn to be on the road in the name of Grace and to see and understand the basic conflict in different areas of the Earth, they learn global compassionate thinking. They also recognize that a conflict which has become global can only be brought to a solution on a holistic level. In

Tamera Healing Biotope I in Portugal a research center arose for international peace forces. Here ecological, social, technological and human knowledge is collected for the realization of real-life peace models. Tamera is in cooperation with peace communities and committed peace workers all over the world. A curriculum has been developed through which the students can study the basics of a new culture. Tamera is a kind of base station for the Global Campus."

Since then, groups and projects which orient themselves on the fundamental thoughts of the Global Campus have been established in many countries. From centers in Colombia, Mexico, Brazil, Israel and Palestine to some groups of the Anastasia movement in Russia to new centers in Portugal and Switzerland, a global network for a free Earth is forming. May a globalization of peace which will be stronger than all violence emerge from the mental-spiritual coherence of these forces. Sabine Lichtenfels writes, *"I am thankful for all forces which helped or will help to build the network. May the cosmic family grow on Earth; may we recognize each other and endow each other with power and hope, even in turbulent times. May we always remember that mighty powers of healing are on our side when we open for them. There is something in all of us which wants to remind us of our very own intact form, as individuals and as humanity. It is the inner God Point (Omega) in all of us, the inner treasure, which now wants to be revealed in ourselves through a great shared planetary action."*

Why Should There Be Such a Project?
We have shed light onto the unspeakable fates of individual humans and animals in the globalized world. Whoever has really borne witness here can never re-

turn to daily routine. The founders of the project were acting out of compassion. The immediate compassion, which we often observe in children and which we all once had, should never become lost, but instead should continuously grow until we have found a solution for how to end the suffering. Thirty four years ago (in May 1978) the "Bauhütte" project was officially founded in Germany, which eventually gave birth to the Tamera project and the plan of the Global Campus. The extent of the global violence demands methods of peace work which extend far beyond all the usual slogans. To this day the co-workers of this project have needed to have a great personal commitment. Why this radical way?

To get straight to the point; as long as there is one single child starving, one single animal tortured, one African girl circumcised, one woman raped, one person of another faith mistreated, one young human being forced to go to war, then our world is in disorder. It is our definite task to free this world from the atrocious pain. We could always say this is an illusion. But as soon as our eyes start to open, as soon as we see the suffering of the victims, as soon as we ourselves are one of these tortured beings, there is only one single cry – the cry for relief.

We are currently experiencing a historical situation: the collapse of the old systems. Human evolution has reached a global dead-end. Fundamental values of community, truth and solidarity have been lost through a millennia-long history of war and the measures of capitalist globalization. The consequences of this maldevelopment are so cruel for the victims on every continent that we have had to close our eyes. The Earth's population lives under a hypnosis of fear and violence.

We can overcome this crisis by giving the coming development a new direction. It is no longer about fighting the existing systems, which will break down by themselves. It is much more about knowing the new directions and creating planetary base stations for them. The Mayan date of December 21, 2012 is not the end of the world, but the beginning of a new era. Millions of young people all over the world who rise up against the old structures need a new answer and a new perspective. Nobody has to starve on our Earth if we use its richness wisely. Food, water and energy are freely available for all of humanity if we develop appropriate structures; these are structures which are no longer oriented around power and profit, but on the common life interest of all inhabitants of Earth, including all animals. We cannot wait until governments make the decisions; we ourselves have to make them. The co-workers of the Global Campus are developing new concepts of living together with animals and plants, of creating an embeddment in nature. They are establishing new projects for the healing of water, for corresponding food biotopes and new models for decentralized energy supply. Above all, they work on new forms of social life including the most intimate realms of sex, love, partnership and community. The Earth needs humans who do not only say what they need, but who do it.

Vera Kleinhammes, the current coordinator of the Global Campus in Tamera writes,

"If young people worldwide can learn to build communities, solve conflicts, practice successful non-violent resistance, if they get reliable knowledge about love, sexuality and partnership, as well as about the most

important issues of ecological sustainability and new energy technologies, food production, healing, network-building and peace journalism, then the necessary globalization of peace will take place. Then we as human beings will be capable of directing the current global transformation in a positive direction."

Community

A central task in our new time is the construction of functioning human communities. The general crisis area of our time is in the relationships amongst humans. Here lies the central switches for war and destruction – or for healing. One of the most important sources for the production of negative or positive energy and information fields is how people treat each other. Especially here, in the realm of underground fears and conflicts, a new course has to be set, the latent wars ended and the psychological mine fields defused. The core issues lie in the areas of sex, love, partnership and community. The many new groups and projects which are currently searching for a new perspective in life will only find calmness if they have found a new orientation in this central area of our human existence. The most intimate questions of life are no longer private problems, but collective issues of humanity.

The communities that form the Global Campus follow certain ethical guidelines for their community life: truth in communication – even in love, mutual support, responsible participation, no abuse of power, readiness for self change, understanding instead of judging, Grace instead of revenge, solidarity with all beings of nature, no violence against animals. It is only possible to really obey these basic rules if all participants are ready for a very intensive change in the habits of their private lives, because we have all learned to lie and to trick in order to make ends meet in our societies. But now communities have to be established where lies and deceit have no evolutionary advantage. We need new social, sexual, economic and mental-spiritual structures, where real trust can emerge: trust between humans and trust in all fellow creatures.

Here the words of Lynn Margulis are appropriate. She says, *"If we wanted to survive the ecological and social crisis which we have caused, we would have to engage in radically new and dramatic community enterprises."*

The coming communities are no longer based on collective ideologies, but on individual insight and decision. One should not carry belief-sentences on one's flag, but work through the thoughts and understand them. Participation in these new communities is not a process of outer conformity, but a process of individuation. Individual autonomy, embedded in a positive community does not lead to anarchy but to participation. A new culture of love, free sexuality and lasting partnerships is the result of following the basic ethical rules as soon as they are adopted in one's core. In a new community, new forms of non-violent cohabitation will develop between human beings, nature and all fellow creatures. All beings – humans, animals, plants and spiritual beings – are part of the community. All partake in the healing fields of energy that are developed in the community. From here, new centers for a future without war will develop – we call them "Healing Biotopes."

Healing of the Waters
"Whoever possesses the secret of water, possesses power."
Viktor Schauberger

The new global society needs a new means of water management. Water is the essence of nature just as love is the essence of the human being. Both areas have been distorted by false information fields. Healing the trauma of water and healing the trauma in love are two basic ways toward a new healed Earth. If we succeed in ending the water catastrophe, the catastrophe of hunger will also come to an end because natural water management is the basis of food supply worldwide. A huge part of the Earth's population lives in indescribable poverty. The misery of hunger is not caused by nature, but is man-made through exploitative land management and catastrophic water management in the name of economic interests. These are system errors, which can be overcome by an all-encompassing system change. This is the reason for our work: to create models for this global system change.

In order to heal the water cycle on a global scale we need so-called Water Retention Landscapes. These are areas which are designed according to principles of landscape healing and which are able to retain all rainwater. The rainwater slowly seeps into the body of the earth, fills up the aquifer and reappears clean in springs. In this way, it does not return back into the rivers and into the global circulation as dirty water carrying the products of erosion, but as fresh spring water. Communities now have clean and energy-rich drinking water. A new form of permaculture will develop around the shores of these water landscapes where a multitude of natural food is grown, such as fruit trees, raspberries, radishes and other regional specialties: a rich biotope which does not need irrigation. A miraculous change in nature, with a lush and growing animal and plant world, takes place in front of our eyes. One starts to learn and understand again what beauty and life-powers nature brings forth as soon as we give her our support.

Many ecological and social movements of our time, such as the Anastasia movement in Russia, could cooperate in the healing of the earth if they would develop two things: a social concept for Eros and community, and an ecological concept based on Water Retention Landscapess and/or landscape healing. This new way of water management especially serves the healing of the landscape and the healing of the water cycle in order to enable a reinhabitation of the land. Rural de-population in the industrial age left vast areas of land uncultivated and led to disastrous population explosions in the metropolitan cities. This fatal process must be reversed if humanity wants to survive. Many people have to return to the land because if we know how to farm it in an intelligent way, everything needed for a good life is provided.

Decentralized rainwater retention could be a key for a global redesign of the earth. Once word has got around, thousands of new groups will move to the countryside in order to build their subsistence economies there. Organic re-cultivation of dry regions (such as the Negev, Portugal, etc.) can now be accomplished with much improved efficiency and with far less technical effort. This will lead to a spectacular revegetation of abandoned and desertified areas of the earth, because nature will support these healing processes with all its power. Water and food is then really available for all human beings. Poor countries could develop self-sufficient food systems which would free them from the despotism of global markets. All those groups which no longer find any perspective in today's city life could actively take part in this process. Soon an interesting regional model could develop in Portugal: "1000 Lakes for the Alentejo." If something like this is really created, the political and economic power structures change on the spot, because the new model demonstrates how easy it is to get out of the grip of the old systems and EU regulations. In order to realize such comprehensive changes in a healing way, they must be connected with the social and ethical conditions that have been described in this manifesto.

Healing of Love
There cannot be peace on Earth as long as there is war in love.

Love follows similar laws as water. Happiness will develop wherever these laws are followed; wherever they are broken, violence arises. Global violence is the result of the fact that for thousands of years the laws of love could not be followed. Present day humanity comes from a several-thousand-year-old history of war, which has left a collective trauma in us all. In this nothing was more terribly hurt than love.

Love, sensual and soul love, is the most important global issue. Sexuality is a world power. The cultural era of our times has failed due to destroyed love and sexual torment. Almost everywhere where there was once love, hatred and violence have developed. The protesters and the policemen who are facing each other worldwide could be friends. The inhabitants of the Colombian peace village San Josécito and their enemies in the paramilitary forces could be friends. Palestinians and Israelis, successors of Ishmael and Israel, could be friends if their loving nature had not been destroyed by insane religious and political education measures. The male aspect of humanity has gone against the commandments of love and sexuality with the commandments of church, state and economy. Where the commandments of love are injured by betrayal and violence, fear of separation develops, along with mistrust, jealousy and hatred. One cannot love any more. One closes the heart once and for all; one starts to hate what one once loved. One fights against a world which one could also embrace. All those who no longer know the power of love choose the power of destruction. This is how the tsunamis of violence develop that have plagued the earth for thousands of years. To a great extent the existing civilization is based on anger and disappointed love. This is not an excessive simplification but the tragic foundation of an era which went wrong.

The new power fields for a healed Earth are the result of a rediscovered joy by people who have found a new form of love and solidarity and whose children have regained a stable home for their souls. Peace work in the outer world can only be successful in the long run if it is connected with peace work in the inner world.

So let's try to develop new life models which are based on joy and fulfilled love – models where Eros is indeed connected to love, because no more lies and no more meanness can sneak in anymore. In Eros lies a key to hell or a key to heaven. We should no longer gamble with this gift given to us by creation. The Global Campus will build retention spaces for water – and retention spaces for love.

Humane Sexual Culture

A cooperation with natural spirits which is free of fear is free of violence. A cooperation with natural spirits which is free of violence is free of fear. To establish a non-violent relationship to nature we must also step into a healthy relationship with our own nature. This is especially true for the issue of sexuality. With all the perspectives we have gained over the inner drives of our earthly existence, we can clearly formulate the following: The historical fight of man against the woman was a fight against his own sexual nature. A new humane culture derives from new relation between the genders and a new ethically and socially responsible use of our sexual powers. A human being who is sexually liberated, capable of love and conscious does not kill life. As soon as the historical trauma of sexual oppression and of oppression of women is resolved, the causes for the unspeakable suffering of peoples, children and all co-creatures will also be resolved.

As long as we have to hide and distort our elementary power, such as we do with sexual desire, we cause energetic disturbances in the system of life. It does not serve healing to suppress the sexual attraction between the genders and to repress our own sexuality. It does not serve healing if we maintain secret relationships and deny them in front of our partners. Nor does it serve healing to follow indiscriminate polygamy in the name of a misunderstood "free sexuality". The world needs a new, humane sexual culture which is based on truth and trust and which enables all participants to again encounter each other in full joy. The world needs an erotic life which is strongly connected to the spirit of the Sacred Matrix and therefore liberates all participants from the chronic fear of loss. A humane sexual culture is based on free sexuality that is not an ideological decision between monogamy and polygamy, but the liberation of sexuality from hypocrisy and meanness. Free sexuality and partnership never exclude each other. Here we are facing the historical situation of the development of a truly new concept of love. The coming planetary society will develop an erotic culture where the sexual attention of one person to another no longer provokes any fear, jealousy or hatred in a third person. Tamera has partly succeeded already in making such a possibility of life visible.

The Sacred Alliance of Life and Cooperation With All Beings of Nature

Healing information fields will develop from a new cooperation with all beings of nature – the material and also non-material beings. In addition to conventional methods, a loving cooperation can also be fostered by more intensive measures, such as the establishment of an animal sanctuary, a specific peace garden (Eike Braunroth), the setting of stones, landscape temples, spiritual power places, crystal patterns and technological devices for the reinforcement and dissemination of new fields. The resonance with the thoughts and actions of the human being is always important here. The thoughts which take effect here are those which Sabine Lichtenfels repeatedly presents in her teachings on the "Prehistoric Utopia" – the inner relationship between all living organisms, the healing significance of snakes, toads, owls and many other animals, the living symbols of the spiritual and cosmic energy system. All of these are part of the great cosmic orchestra. All of them enthusiastically take part in the process of global healing.

Many of Tamera's co-workers came from helping professions. But in a system where the most cruel actions take place a million times every day, helping in a single situation is like a drop in a bucket. In Tamera, for example, we had a problem with dogs which were injured and abused and came to us searching for protection. We helped as much as we could, but the animal suffering which became visible was too much. Neither was it enough to ask local authorities nor animal welfare organizations for their support. We need a higher level of help for all living beings, for humans as well as for animals. This will be achieved when we develop a new model for living that has a global effect, in which cruelty against co-creatures no longer exists because new information lines for a non-violent life have been manifested. This is the underlying thought.

Arteries of water run through the earth. Can we cooperate with water? Can we make it an ally for global peace work? The world's oceans cover 70% of the earth's surface. They hold an inexhaustible world of wildlife. Can we cooperate with the inhabitants of the oceans? Can we make them into allies for global peace work?

The material world, including our atmosphere with its weather cycles, is filled with streaming vital life energies. Can we cooperate with them? Can we make them allies for global peace work?

The plants and trees of the earth are beings with a soul. Can we cooperate with them? Can we make them allies for global peace work? The so-called vermin in our gardens are part of the one big family of life. Can we cooperate with snails, voles, aphids etc.? Can we make them allies for global peace work? (We refer to the amazing experiences in the peace gardens of Eike Braunroth.)

Snakes and rats also belong to the Sacred Matrix. For thousands of years they were frightening spirits to the human being. Can we cooperate with them? Can we make them allies for global peace work? From our years of experience in Tamera we can answer this question with a definite "YES."

This is what we mean when we use the term "cooperation with nature." It is about winning the whole of nature as an ally for global healing. It may sound like science fiction, but it is more than this, because it is part of the blueprint of creation. All beings on Earth are organs of the One body and minds of the One spirit.

The Theoretical Matrix of the Project

The Global Campus is a sign of a planetary system change from the matrix of violence to the matrix of the Global Alliance with all beings. In order to free the Earth from violence and war we need to turn on a global switch. It is this switch which will decide whether holograms of fear and violence or holograms of trust and cooperation will be downloaded from the cosmic database. The cosmic database contains both possibilities, as it is in the genetic material of the human being. From this cosmic database we can activate the old information from the millennia of war or the new information for a healthy Earth. This is what we do with every thought and every action of our daily life. Human behavior is steered – as is very likely the behavior of everything in the universe – by invisible fields of energy and information. If we succeed in changing the information patterns in core areas of our existence then we send new information into the biological Internet, which will bring about fundamental changes in life on the whole planet. In this way it is easily conceivable that a planetary human society could develop whose participants are no longer psychologically or physiologically predisposed to any violent actions because they no longer receive impulses that steer them in this direction. They live in a different hologram. From the many possibilities in the cosmic database, a world of healing love and solidarity has manifested itself. It may sound like a dream, but it is an achievable reality. *"What can be thought, can be done,"* said Einstein. These are very briefly the theoretical guidelines of our work. (They are definitely not complete, and you will find deeper information in the writings of Dieter Duhm.)

The theoretical concept has been developed out of a long period of research, and today forms the basis of our actions. The message is clear. The fight between the forces of life and the forces of destruction can be decided clearly in favor of life if we make the necessary ecological, social and ethical decisions. The losers of yesterday can be the winners of tomorrow. But strictly speaking, there will no longer be any more losers if humanity changes its orientation from power and profit to the universal laws of life and the higher-level structure that is inherent in all things in the universe, which we call the "Sacred Matrix." The "global players" of the new era no longer think about revenge and retaliation, for they work in their centers and within themselves to build structures of peace. "Grace" is their watchword. It is not only about ending violence and war, but also about changing the underlying conditions that repeatedly give rise to violence. Fear is the one condition which, more than any other, underlies all systems of injustice. Eduar Lanchero is one of the spokespersons of the well-known peace community San José de Apartadó in Colombia. In the past years almost 200 members of the community have been cruelly murdered by the military and paramilitary. During a meeting of the Global Campus he said,

"The armed groups are not the only ones who kill. It is the logic behind the whole system. The way people live generates this kind of death. This is why we decided to live in a way that our life generates life. One basic condition, which kept us alive was to not play the game of fear, which was imposed upon us by the murders of the armed forces. We have made our choice. We chose life. Life corrects us and guides us."

It belongs to the system of the Global Campus to support such peace communities by all means of friendship, cooperation and concrete human and technological aid. *"Fear must disappear from Earth,"* said Michael Gorbachov. We try to create the right preconditions for this with all scientific, technological, social and spiritual measures we know.

Global Extension

The theoretical matrix leads to a new model for global extension. It does not consist of global missionary work, nor of elaborate public relations maneuvres, but in the functional logic of holistic systems. Publicity happens "automatically" if the work complies with the internal laws of the universal matrix. (This is the reason the Tamera project was able to survive until today despite all attacks.) As soon as the first models are functioning, they will develop all over the world, because their new information fields are global fields, stored in the cosmic database and engraved in the genetic matrix of life on Earth. When the core information of trust and solidarity is activated in a population, a switch will happen in all other areas of life as well. A general opening of all channels will take place, which so far have been blocked by fear. The information will spread by itself through the biological Internet where it is transferred as a "holo-wave" or "carrier-wave" to all participants. From this concept we can understand why local actions can bring about global effects. A decision we make here and now can result in a chain reaction of new decisions in other places on Earth. The laws of field-building processes in holistic systems are operating here. Only a few decades into the 21st century, our children and grandchildren will know the atrocities of the imperialistic war history only from their textbooks. The change will take place fast. We stand right before the boiling point of a planetary revolution. Peace work today is the active and conscious participation in this global process.

A Final Comment
For some readers this project may at first seem illusory; wireless Internet also seemed illusory once. It is only a wall of old thinking habits which separates us from new possibilities. The project is based on research and community experience, which we undertook over a period of 34 years in a growing community that today has 170 participants in Germany and Portugal. We found that guidance overlaid all developments, which always led us on new paths. Today we are inclined to say that it actually was not us who invented this project, but we were somehow driven to do it. It represents a new direction in evolution, which is being prepared everywhere today. The leading forces are forces of global transformation, in which the basic forms of the Sacred

Matrix manifest themselves on Earth. The groups and projects which take a stand for life in the present system-change are cooperating with high powers and are therefore under high protection. The movement can no longer be stopped. Behind all turbulences a new planetary community will arise, where violence is no longer an option. At its center is the rediscovered unity of all life and solidarity with all creatures. At the very core is the rediscovered light of the source from which we all originate. We have reached the threshold of a global change of un-imaginable extent.

THE EARTH NEEDS NEW INFORMATION

Monika Alleweldt, 2013

"We must use all the available options which have been given to us to end global suffering."
Dieter Duhm

Humankind's dream of a world without war and violence must become more than a dream. According to psychoanalyst and project founder, Dr. Dieter Duhm, and his team, the realization of this dream is a realistic undertaking. Based on their 30 years of research and experience in the development of projects which explore issues related to the future of humanity, they have developed what is called a "Political Theory." This theory forms the basis for an extraordinary peace plan, which has already been implemented in its basic form. This peace plan is now facing a new level of actualization, which urgently needs global attention. The Earth's crisis has become so blatant that it is absolutely vital that we spread the knowledge about freeing our planet from the grip of violence.

For most of us, the contention that peace can arise on this war-torn planet in the foreseeable future lies so far outside the realm of possibility, that we would not even give it a second thought. However, just a few decades ago, almost nobody could have imagined wireless Internet and the Hubble telescope in outer space. Serious work is being done today on the colonization of Mars, including plans for the transformation of the Martian atmosphere (terra-forming). Humankind could obviously use the same intelligence that leads to the conception of these types of technical achievements to work on the question of how fear and violence could be made to vanish from the Earth. It is only a question of our will and our focus. As a matter of fact, if we cannot find an answer to the problem of violence on Earth, we can only hope to find its fatal continuation on Mars.

New ideas release new potential for action. Grand theories are paving the way for great revolutions. We would like to thank all those who are willing to carefully study and understand this theory. When this type of new idea enters into the dialogue, we will have taken the first step toward ensuring that this peace plan is successful. This document contains the thoughts that led to the development of the Political Theory and the resulting peace plan. For a full understanding of the theory, further reading would be necessary. A list of recommended reading materials can be found at the end of the book.

Compassion for the World

The political theory was born from compassion. The power of the mind and that of the heart have become so coupled in this political theory that there is a clear vision of the potential for effective action and assistance. Compassion with what is happening in the world is a key to understanding the theory. At the same time, compassion is also a key to personal healing. The healing of the world coincides with individual healing.

In his book, "Future Without War," Dieter Duhm writes, *"In many regions of the world today, there is suffering which we can no longer perceive with any clarity. We are no longer able to react when we hear what people do to each other, what they do to children, what they are doing to all the peoples and what they do to animals. The atrocities are too harrowing to be let into the soul. We know that it happens on every continent, but we no longer react to it. It has taken on an abstract, formal dimension."*

A collective habit of separation and suppression has become widespread. We take refuge in our private existence and no longer seek a global solution. If this continues, the "Brave New World" would be definitively established, and the millions of beings that are tortured, mutilated, enslaved, imprisoned, starving and dying of thirst will have lost their last hope. If we do not want this, we need to preserve within ourselves the power and the ability to sympathize with the world, including the fate of both the victims and the perpetrators, without succumbing to fear or resignation. We need to open our hearts in order to be able to work toward a new future. We need to have a realistic perspective on how to end this global misery.

Accordingly, Neale Donald Walsch writes in his book, "Conversations with God," that from the day we really become willing to end world hunger, there will be no more hunger in the world. *"You have chosen not to do it."* It is our choice as to which issues we deal with on a daily basis. It is our choice which targets we aim for. At the moment in which we truly want to end war on Earth, we will find a way.

The Changing Times

We find ourselves in a period of transformation from a materialistic age in which individual things or events are in the foreground, to an era in which all individual things and events are united by vibration, frequency and information. This union will be humanity's new focus. It is not the atom, but rather information that is the building block of the material world, "In the beginning was the Word." Human behavior, like probably everything else in the universe, is controlled by invisible energy and information fields. The Earth with its mountains and oceans, its flora and fauna, people and cultures, is a uniform, vibrating body of life. There is something that is the same in everything. We can study the flow of life everywhere, in streams or in the bark of a tree, in a shell, or in our own bodies. Everything has emerged from one creative impulse, which vibrates and resonates with great cosmic rhythms and pulses, which make our heart beat, organizes our thoughts and animates all life. It is a deep, calm vibration. Hence the mantra: from calmness comes power. Athletes experience it when they are in the "zone." Those who are connected to this power can "move mountains."

The unity of the world and the unity of all beings have been repeatedly experienced by religious mystics who have described it in a language of vibrant, ecstatic colors. Today, this unity is conveyed in the sober language of science, across many disciplines from quantum physics to holography. In a similar way, our body is a unified organism, made up of various organs and cells, coordinated by an invisible "headquarters." Every second, billions of high-precision molecular interactions take place in our cells without us needing to be even slightly aware of it. It is worth pausing here and really taking note of this "miracle."

It is the self-organizing principle of life, which we can see manifested here in our earthly, individual body. In the same way that our organs perform specialized roles in our body to create a functional whole, the human race has its special task in the blueprint of creation.

In the long run, it is impossible for humanity to work against this plan.

Become a Cooperation Partner in Service of Life

Through the global chain of fear and violence, wars and genocides, and through the destruction of nature and its creatures, humankind has spread a hard and destructive interference frequency above the Earth, which isolates him to a certain degree from the self-organizing information field of life. The original, unified world is now severely disrupted and superimposed upon by this disturbing frequency. This allows our society to be controlled by systems that follow the principles of profit, domination and exploitation, even though they blatantly violate the logic of life and nature. The global problems of our time are the result of this collision between the man-made system of capitalism and the natural system of life.

In every moment, with every thought, word and action, we decide what information will be sent into the world and whether we stand on the side of fear and violence or on the side of healing and trust. The choice is ours. Peace Pilgrim says, *"Speak, think and act in such a way that peace arises within you."* This is a new form of peace activism. In every moment we manage turn the "switch" in the direction of trust, we create an escape route from this global suffering. Everything is a continuum. Life needs all human cooperation partners who recognize this logic. *"If life wins, there will be no losers"* (D. Duhm).

All over the world, solutions to the problems of our time are being developed. There are solutions that would allow the world's water crisis to be healed within a few years and all living beings could be supplied with ample drinking water. Heavily polluted water can also be cleaned. Wherever the water problem can be solved, a viable solution to the world hunger problem is in sight. There are also solutions through which local measures could prevent the imminent climate collapse. In addition, there are solutions to the question of whether a global energy supply can be created purely by means of renewable resources, without the use of fossil fuels.

For the most part, these individual pieces of information work against the interests of capitalist globalization and are therefore structurally suppressed. The consciousness of the world, despite the multitude of solutions, continues to be characterized by scarcity thinking, futility and helplessness. We need to turn these individual pieces of information into one coherent system of information. They are like the pieces of a puzzle. If we put these pieces together correctly we can see the whole picture, the dream of humanity. If we succeed in making this visible in different places on Earth, it will spark hope and spread as unstoppably as any idea whose time has come.

Until then, we need an alliance of intelligent people to spread a higher frequency, a stream of care, a vibration of compassion and unity throughout the world and to teach people about this carrier frequency and its corresponding content. They cannot fail to soften the hard disturbance frequency. Heart tones must be heard again, a recognizable perspective that could provide a new direction for our resistances and protests, for our power and love. *The Earth needs new information.*

For this, we need above all, beyond technical and financial support, beyond even political and spiritual protection, a global approach.

A Global Concept of Peace

"You never change things by fighting the existing reality. To change something, build a new model that makes the existing model obsolete."
Buckminster Fuller

Dieter Duhm and his team developed the idea to realize a future peace society by first developing a model. Just as in industry, prototypes are built before the product goes into production. In this context, the prototypes are special research centers, so-called Healing Biotopes. In these centers, corresponding individual solutions are implemented, linked with each other and further developed. In this way, a complex aggregate of information, the image of a global culture of peace, comes into being.

The Political Theory explains why the presence of just a few Healing Biotopes on Earth could be enough to cause a global change from the previous system of violence to a new era of peace. Accordingly, this peace plan provides for the establishment of these centers. The first model of this type, the Tamera Peace Research Center in Portugal, was founded in 1995 by Dieter Duhm, Sabine Lichtenfels and others and now has approximately 170 co-workers. The work at Tamera has resulted in the emergence of an "Institute for Global Peace Work," a "Political Ashram," a Water Retention Landscape, regional self-sufficiency, permaculture, a "Solar Village," an animal sanctuary, a children's republic, an open school, an international training platform (Global Campus and Terra Nova School), an arts and healing center, a Global Love School and more. Groups in Israel-Palestine, Colombia, Mexico and other countries are preparing to build similar models. The project is clearly on its way to realization, but there is still much to do. From "Future Without War," come the thoughts,

"What is decisive for the success of such peace projects is not how big and strong they are (compared to the existing apparatuses of violence), but how comprehensive and complex they are, how many elements of life they combine and unite in themselves in a positive way. In the field buildings of evolution it is not the "survival of the fittest" but the "success of the more comprehensive." Otherwise, no new development would have been able to impose itself, for they all began as "small and inconspicuous."

At the heart of this peace plan is new information, the image of a realistic alternative way of life. We would like to demonstrate the power of such an image with the example of a case that the Russian healer and physician Arkady Petrov tells of in his book "The Creation of the World – Part I." (We ask you not to get too caught up in whether or not you believe in this type of healing. Our chief concern is also not about the work of certain doctors or healers. The experience described should speak for itself.)

A Healing Experience

As Denis A. is admitted to the Moscow hospital after a serious car accident, the doctors give him hardly any chance of survival. Arkady Petrov is consulted. He rushes to the intensive care unit with his two young assistants. The assistants, who are gifted with clairvoyance, put on blindfolds and look intuitively upon the serious injuries. Petrov writes,

"Denis' consciousness is almost completely extinguished. He does not want to bear the pain; he does not want to live; he does not know what he has to live for. For me and

47

my assistants, this means that Denis must first remember the goal of his existence, his purpose, so that he will want to fight for his life. But how can this be done? The girls see a luminous image in Denis' consciousness – a small infant. They enlarge the image. Denis has recently had a daughter. His love for her could be the purpose of his life. They reinforce the hologram energetically. Denis' brain impulses slowly begin to strengthen. Suddenly, Denis begins to cry, strange as it may seem for a man who is in a coma to be able to cry."

An extraordinary healing process begins. The girls accompany this healing process around the clock. After two weeks, Denis opens his eyes again. He is still unable to speak, but confirms with a squeeze of the hand that he is getting better. Some time later, his condition has improved so much that he is discharged from the hospital.

Activation of the Original Matrix

Denis' healing was made possible by a picture in his soul, which made him want to fight for his life. It was a picture of his love. Through this picture, his will to live was awakened, and a potential capable of releasing great healing powers was activated. It was this information that made the choice between life and death.

We can transfer this process from the individual to humankind and assume that, here too, a guiding piece of information, or as indigenous peoples say, a "dream," is at the center and could have a similar significance for the development of humankind and the Earth.

When Lynne Twist, from the United States, met representatives of the Achua, (one of the last pristine tribes of the Amazon at that time,) in the Ecuadorian rainforest, the natives pleaded with her, *"If you want to help us, do not come to us. Go back to your world and change the dream of your culture. It is because of that, that we are perishing."* Lynne Twist returned and founded the Pachamama Alliance, an organization with which, to this day, she educates hundreds of thousands of people through global associations and demonstrates alternatives with the aim of changing the "dream" of capitalism.

Today even governments, such as the (indigenous) governments of Bolivia and Ecuador, are developing the concept of another dream. They call it "Buen Vivir" or "Vivir Bien" (Good Living). The concept invokes indigenous traditions and values. However, it so far exists only in written form. Therefore, globalization can further infiltrate in Bolivia. (We wish that Bolivia employs model thinking to support the development of "Vivir Bien" in a way that is applicable for everyday life).

Russian author Vladimir Megre longs for a simple, almost religious life in the countryside, which he so aptly illustrated in his "Anastasia" books. Millions of young Russians, having been inspired, left their jobs in the cities to move to the countryside. They have begun to establish the external conditions of life that correspond to the principles of "Anastasia." Now, the first of them are faced with the question of how they can change their internal conditions in such a way that how they live together is determined by solidarity and commonality.

The Dutch sociologist, politician and futurist Fred Polak showed that a positive image of the future is the most important factor determining the rise and fall of civilizations ("The Image of the Future," 1973).

The above are just a few examples of the power and importance of motivational imagery.

In the present context, the key questions include: How might an image that inspires the whole of humanity look? For which image would humanity struggle for its own survival and for the survival of the entire planet? For what goal would we leave all disputes behind in order to succeed with united vigor?

In the logic of the Political Theory, we can say that, first of all, such a picture can only replace the existing image if it does not simply negate the prior one, but is integrated at a higher level. Secondly, the new image must be internally consistent. Thirdly, it must, at least in the initial stages, be put into practice in a tangible manner. It has to work. This realization must take place within the context of several exemplary pilot projects throughout the world so that the image can achieve global validity.

Imagine if there were this healing image that could be used to activate the "original matrix of humankind," and in so doing, activate the collective healing potential of this matrix. From one day to the next, humankind would begin to work toward healing instead of toward destruction. People would agree, for example, to use the global military expenditure from now on for the restoration of the oceans, for the re-greening of the deserts, for the protection of all animals, for the development of modern subsistence economies, for energy from inexhaustible sources, for solar powered vehicles, for schools in which sympathy and love is taught (including sensual love), for a new religion free of punishment and purgatory, which encourages people to create paradise on Earth rather than placing it in the sky.

The Earth would be completely transformed within a very short time.

Knowledge is available, or could be further developed and elaborated on in each of the above areas in a short time. So why is it that we lack the faith to be able to actualize an ideal world? Modern man does not doubt in technology. Because of it, almost anything is possible. But when it comes to peace, to an agreement among people for a common goal, then we quickly reach our limit of the thinkable. Why has humankind not already found the healing information long ago?

The Collective Trauma

Dieter Duhm is a sociologist and psychoanalyst, and was one of the leaders of the German Left at the time of the '68 student movement. His book, "Fear in Capitalism" was published in 1972 and became a bestseller. He combined therein his psychoanalytical knowledge of internal human processes with the question of how an external global revolution could succeed. He described "collective trauma," a deep-rooted fear in the subconscious of every human being, and beyond that, applied this individual interpretation to a historical context. Through the millennia-long history of violence, this fear pervades human con-sciousness like an invisible nervous system.

So that this trauma is not repeated, humans have developed a vast array of defense mechanisms that are activated every time we approach the point of fear. Our daily lives, our conversations, our political views, and our love relationships are penetrated by this explosive and irrational defensive behavior. This irrational be-havior shatters the most beautiful utopias. This un-conscious trauma can transform a great love into a nerve-wracking, long-term war. The whole world is perishing today because of it.

One of the most fatal strategies is transferring our fear to a convenient external object rather than resolving it in ourselves. This is why we create images of enemies that can be fought. This provides short-term relief, but increases our anxiety immeasurably in the long run. Our projection of fear is why our environment, our fellow human beings, and even our love partner can seem potentially threatening. The trauma controls us if we orient our entire lives toward an imaginary penal authority and adapt to social conditions we do not like, rather than realizing the dreams of our youth.

Fear comes from constriction and acts like an explosive residue, which can erupt at any time as anger, hatred, jealousy, sadism, and unconcealed violence. *"War lives secretly within every peace,"* the poet Hermann Hesse once said. It was this collective trauma that transformed brave fathers into concentration camp executioners overnight. It is collective trauma that makes us deeply corruptible. If this long-term unconscious fear, and the consequent latent propensity for violence, did not exist inside every man, then a handful of rulers would never be able to maneuver the whole of the Earth's population toward its own demise. We now understand why we will always lose the fight against external imperialist power, as long as we do not also resolve the stronghold of this power which lives within us. This is how Dieter Duhm was able to say in the 60's, *"Revolution without emancipation is counterrevolution."* Or today, *"A revolution cannot succeed on the outside unless it has also taken place on the inside."*

The new information that is being sought lies behind the walls of this trauma. This is why it seems so elusive.

This is why it cannot just be laid out on the drawing board, but requires places of healing where this trauma can be resolved by the first human examples.

New Information and the Building of Revolutionary Healing Centers

Karl Marx said that the social being determines the consciousness of men. In this regard, Dieter Duhm has remained a Marxist when he says that the resolution of trauma requires a new "social being." He removes the concept of "healing" from the therapeutic context and places it at the center of a revolutionary movement. The sought after healing community cannot come to fruition through appeals, laws, reforms or party platforms. The trauma cannot be healed through those types of measures. Moreover, the new paradigms should definitely be discovered and mutually agreed upon first.

The centers will be established by people who are ready for radical self-transformation and self-revelation. They will not be doing it only for themselves; that could never succeed at all. They will be doing it on behalf of all humankind. They will explore trust: the elixir, out of which a new world emerges. Trust between men and women, adults and children, the human being and nature, individual and community. Where this trust is restored, the seeds of crystallization for a new future emerge. All areas of life are included in the research and removed from the pattern of violence, from the external necessities of life such as water, food and energy to the inner sources of art, community, religion and Eros.

The new image cannot simply be arbitrarily conceived and imposed on humanity. It is rather a latent human dream which wants to be rediscovered, so beautiful and primal that hardly anyone dares to believe in it. It is the dream of a world without war, in which the great reconciliation has taken place between all those who once stood against each other as enemies, a reconciliation between peoples and religions, between man and woman, between humans and nature.

To rekindle belief in this image, three source areas must be reconnected within the people and within their culture: religion, nature and Eros. Our love for religion, our origins, the light, and the world of the mind and spirit must be able to reconnect with our love of nature, with all its crawling, grunting, and waddling creatures to its flowers, scents and fruits to its rivers and seas, valleys and mountains. Both religion and nature must be able to reconnect with our love for people, above all with our love for the opposite gender, for man and woman, for flesh, for pleasure, for delight, for matter.

Where these three areas (religion, nature and Eros) of our existence can come back into alignment, the human heart can heal; a heart which has for so long been torn asunder. A new humanity, matured through the painful experience of a long history of war, in which they were personally involved, can be resurrected, set upright by its rediscovered faith in itself, strengthened by its absolute and unconditional NO to any form of violence.

Now we have arrived at the source point from which a future without war may be developed. From now on, the world that has created us can shine a light on the world that we create; it can be reflected in our thoughts and actions, our gardens and fields, our culture and technology, our communities and love relationships. From now on, we are in resonance with a great power and elemental force. From now on, "We gather all the information that we need, to develop our gifts for the benefit of all," as Dhyani Ywahoo said. From now on, we are no longer under the spell of horror and war, but in the service of care for everything that has skin and fur.

In "Future Without War," Dieter Duhm writes, *"The main problem is not the question of whether the new centers can be globally effective, but whether we are in a position to create them. Precisely because they are a part of the whole, the burden of the whole depends on them. They can only succeed if they can arrive at the "universal common ground" that they share with the whole. That universal ground is the invulnerable basis of all human beings, their common source and dowry, their divine core. It shows itself in the capacity for truth, for love and for the recognition of a higher order of life. The new communities begin to have a global effect when they have found the dimension in the fabric of humanity, in which all the Earth's inhabitants are connected with each other and with all living creatures. This is the basis upon which the fragments of life that had been separated for so long merge and unite: man and woman, person and person, spirit and sexuality, Eros and Agape, human being and nature, human being and God. This demonstrates the indispensable spiritual dimension of future healing work. Healing is a return from exile, the lifting of the primal pain that persisted in separation."*

A Transmitting Station for Peace
In order to continue this work in a meaningful way, it must be made known to a wider public. *"The Earth needs new information,"* on this first and most obvious level, means that humankind must learn of this endeavor. Knowledge of how to build a new future must reach all the people who seek it. They must learn how they can eliminate their material and psychological

distress and contribute to a world without war. Then, they will have found a direction that is worth surviving for.

There must be cooperation between those who establish Healing Biotopes, and those who continue to work in society and want to support and protect the centers from the outside. Thus, a new communication network has come into being. This includes potentially everyone, as logically there is no outward border. Everyone can participate in building this shared dream.

We are faced with the task of constructing a first "transmitting station for peace," within the nascent Tamera Healing Biotope, in order to communicate the global peace plan around the world. This transmitting station includes various subdivisions.

We have launched the "Terra Nova School," which provides study material for all those who wish to establish support bases for this dream in their countries. The school offers a vast and beautiful curriculum. It is composed of the following three areas of study: Cooperation with Nature, Learning to Love, and New Thinking. Its study material ranges from blueprints for biogas plants, to new thoughts on love, partnership and sexuality, to study texts on various aspects of a new worldview. The lessons are provided at no charge or on donation via the Internet.

The "Global Campus" takes on the task of providing further practical training, with the particular goal of guiding groups who want to build more research centers like this.

The media affairs department, "Grace Media," conveys the basic ideas and results in the form of video clips, short films and instructional videos. The "political art" group will illustrate the desired future in emblems, text panels, posters, paintings and sculptures. Books and study texts on various topics are published by "Verlag Meiga." "Writers for Peace" is a group of journalists who disseminate the new information through blogs, commentaries and articles.

In anticipation of the future.

II THE HEALING OF LOVE

COMMUNITY AS A RESEARCH SUBJECT

Excerpt from the Project Declaration I

Dieter Duhm, 2005

Happiness is being at home in something greater.

The fulfillment of life also depends on how I answer the question: For whom or what are you doing all this? If the answer is convincingly directed towards something greater than one's own person, a fulfilled life could be in sight. Solving personal problems requires a higher level of order. Such a higher level of order is community. Community means living on a communitarian, rather than a private basis. The mental and moral shift from a private to a communitarian way of life may be one of the most radical paradigm shifts. It is only in this way that we can permanently dismantle the mechanisms of protection and defense with which the isolated human beings of our time have had to familiarize themselves. The Healing Biotopes Project has suffered some massive strokes of fate in its 25 year history. How did the community survive them? It survived because it had developed a stable energy field that held the participants together. The participants were already sufficiently familiar with the rules of a communitarian way of life so as to not fall into individual resignation.

Community means to really get to know other people and see who they really are. We gradually enter the human world that lies beyond the facade of fiction. Here, we find real encounters from center to center and from truth to truth, and the result is genuine trust. Trust is the most original and most efficient of all healing forces. The very first task of a community is therefore to create trust amongst the participants. Can we sense what this means? Do we know how many wedges were driven between human beings during the patriarchal era – between man and woman, parents and children, young and old, peoples and cultures? The task of re-establishing lost original trust is equivalent with the task of activating completely new chains of information in the genetic code of humanity. Old patterns of conduct must be abandoned and replaced by new ones. It is a learning process beyond comparison.

Is Elisabeth Kübler-Ross incorrect when she says that all learning processes in life have the end result of having to learn to love?

And should we not be able to do that?

Let us look at this question from a greater distance. Humanity has built stations in space, invented self-guiding missiles, deciphered the genetic code and shot at cancer cells with nano-cannons – should it not be able to solve its inner problems with the same effort and the same persistence?

THERE WILL BE NO PEACE ON EARTH AS LONG AS THERE IS WAR IN LOVE

Manifesto for the Founding of the Global Love School

Sabine Lichtenfels, 2013

Love and sexuality are a political issue to which we will no longer close our eyes.

Love is more than a feeling. Social vessels are required to allow love to be lived and made real.

It requires a system of ethics in which we can become genuine.

Independent of the question of what our personal lives look like right now and independent of whether we live alone or in community – celibate, married, monogamous, or polygamous – we are working together towards perspectives for our children, and for the generations that will come after us.

We need answers in love so that children can once again grow up in trust and can find home. We need answers that are stronger than all our fear, that awaken desire and curiosity in us, instead of awakening the fear that we will yet again be hurt in these very sensitive areas of love.

Free Eros and partnership are not mutually exclusive. On the contrary – they complement one another. Truth in love is the basis for every lasting love relationship. The question of whether we want to live in monogamy or polyamory, heterosexuality or homosexuality, is decided on the basis of our inner truth.

It is not a contradiction to long for a partner and at the same time to long for erotic adventures. It only becomes betrayal when we have to conceal it from our partners! There is a fidelity in which the devotion of one love partner to another does not trigger fear of loss, but instead brings joy and growth in Eros and trust.

When we have this experience we will wake up one day and say that war is not our adventure anymore. Love is. Eros has become our sacred wellspring of life and of love.

Our sexuality is again anchored in the universal order of life. It is sacred to us, as sacred as life itself.

A new erotic culture will arise from this, in which war will become unthinkable. We see the possibility of ending the war in love, thus introducing entirely new ways of living together and new social structures. Love is the power for the germination of a new culture of peace, based not on sacrifice but rather affirming life's abundance.

Here is a buried, but clearly visible escape from the dead-end street of our time. It leads to a culture of partnership, in which no mother has to send her son to war, in which no father has to surrender his life to defend his country. There will be no more Ministries of Defense. Military bases will be turned into Peace Universities, where the protection of this planet can be learned and practiced.

Love and sexuality must be learned by every adult human being who wants to become a responsible member of this culture.

Lovers and gardeners of a new Earth – Terra Nova – are emerging, where Eros and lasting love are given another chance.

THE IMPORTANCE OF A GLOBAL LOVE SCHOOL

Free Speech given by Sabine Lichtenfels for the Opening
of the Global Love School

Sabine Lichtenfels, 2013

A very warm welcome to the planetary community.
This is the day I have long been waiting for – the beginning of the Global Love School.

Whenever I speak publicly about love and sexuality,
my whole body is in turmoil. I feel the connection
to the size and depth of the topic, but I also feel the
connection to what is happening in this moment with
so many women and men around the world who are
suffering from the effects of misdirected, oppressed
and misguided love and sexuality. We are trying to
figure out how to heal these wounds in Tamera. We
seek healing, not only in our own hearts and our own
relationships, but as an example for the world.

Love and sexuality are a political issue. There is an
emergency call on Earth. It is an emergency call to end
the war in love. War in love is the underground upon
which all violence, every struggle amongst people and
every war finds its sustenance, be it with words, with
thoughts, or ultimately, with weapons. The answer can
only be given collectively, not privately.

Not long ago, we received a letter from a friend who
had to witness a husband beating his wife to death out
of jealousy on the streets of his city.

Last winter there were riots in India in protest of the
rape and murder of a young woman on a bus. Countless
women and girls are raped every day, but this one case
caused a global outcry. Sitting amongst us are people

who have contributed to the subsequent global action to end the violence.

How can we actually stop the violence, not only as an appeal, but in reality? We are dealing with this question in the Global Love School and I'm glad that we can now work together.

Healing Through Information
Do we have an answer that we can really believe in? Which fundamental ideas of the Global Love School do we all share?

The participants of the Global Love School agree that a change in this world is necessary. They realize that one reason for the violence and unresolved issues of civilization lies in misdirected, blocked and suppressed love and sexuality. The participants of the Global Love School realize that the Earth needs new information in this area, because they know that information can lead to healing.

In the Global Love School, we are looking for answers that go beyond the personal, answers that are global in their implications. We are looking for answers that will work anywhere... in India, in South America, in Western culture and in indigenous cultures. Is there something that has gone wrong across all these cultures... something that needs healing everywhere on the planet?

I would like to be very careful about this. I have studied theology. As a young woman I heard how much suffering the Church brought to the world through its missionary work, and I was shocked. Missionaries have often disseminated their ideas not with compassion and mindfulness, but in a patronizing and disrespectful manner, and have forcefully advanced in places where they were not welcome. This is why I am always very conscious of the question, 'What does it mean to think globally and not missionize?'

It is a distinct characteristic of the Global Love School to first go in full awareness and mindfulness, and then to ask what really brings healing from this attitude. When we touch on the issues of love and sexuality in this way, we ask ourselves, 'To what extent are we willing to look at ourselves? Are we ready to include our own personal issues in the research? Are we ready to understand that our personal questions are not private?' Experiences that we perceive as deeply personal, are experienced by people in other places in exactly the same way. Pain, abandonment and betrayal in love form a field, an underground, that often lingers in the unconscious but leads to thoughts and actions in all people which shape our present culture of war. And yet, we generally consider it to be private.

It is therefore important that we in the Global Love School lift our personal issues onto a global level. It is equally important that we know, and do not conceal, the fact that we do not have all the answers. It is essential for us to be willing to ask questions and see their necessity.

In the Global Love School we want to work on an objective ethic for love, on an orientation that we can give ourselves and others. One of the first guidelines is that we are often the best teachers in the areas that we most urgently need to learn ourselves. Therefore, it is necessary to be in touch with ourselves; we cannot afford to ignore our weak points. Only then can we create transparency in the places where we live and work. Then we can say things like, "Jealousy does not belong to love." I can say that, even if I myself am very jealous. I need not and should not hide it. I must not pretend that I have already solved everything. No – I can wholeheartedly say that I am jealous. But I see that I am not in a state of love when I am jealous. I see that jealousy is a disease and I would like to heal it.

New Social Structures –
Jealousy Does Not Belong to Love
In the Global Love School, the topic of love and sexuality does not refer to personal therapy. It is rather about finding the applicable social structures in which healing can take place. More than our personal failures and imperfections, it is our social structures that cause the breakdown of so many love stories.

What forms of cohabitation support love? How can we live, exchange with each other and be together in such a way that it is no longer necessary to lie? How can a life look in which lying to our partners no longer brings us benefit?

These days we find it quite normal not to tell the truth in a love relationship. People all over the world also consider it normal to hide their sexual impulses and desires because of shame. Can we visualize a form of social interaction in which we can joyfully make everything visible and transparent without fear of condemnation, and where we can support each other in the process?

The topic of new social structures very clearly shows us once again that healing in love is a political issue.

If we see the hope that is triggered in people by our Water Retention Landscape or the answers that are developed here in Tamera, in the field of technology for example, then we can see that we have to find solutions for the issue of love with the same power and intensity, so that environmental and technological models do not break down because of interpersonal conflicts. In order to build Water Reten- tion Landscapes and decentralized energy systems, we also need to know how communities emerge that build and live with them.

A Water Retention Landscape forms a biotope by itself. A wide variety of plants and animals make their appearance and great biological diversity arises. Based on these processes, we can study life itself and realize that we are part of nature. If we wish to protect nature, we cannot leave out the topic of human nature. We can best protect nature outside by recognizing, respecting and humanizing our inner nature, including our wild nature, so that it is not destructive but intervenes in a helpful and nurturing manner.

We can also learn how to develop in love through communication with nature, with water and with plants and animals.

Faithfulness and Freedom in Love

In today's society, love and sexuality are organized so that they are permissible within the context of part-nership, but if you take it outside, you are cheating on your partner. Why is that?

Can we not imagine a way of living together where I am fully faithful to my partner and nevertheless may enter into erotic adventures? Could this not be normal in a healthy society, so that we need not fear losing our partner or believe that we should leave them if we love and desire someone else?

Liz Taylor once said in a television interview, "If he takes up with someone else, I'll kill him." And the audience perceived this as evidence of true, passionate love. What insanity! The models that have been presented to us through our upbringing and through the media have conditioned us to believe that passionately expressed jealousy is an expression of love.

Couldn't a completely different picture emerge? When my partner tells me that he feels attracted to another woman, can this not be an indication of how intense and good our partnership is? When he comes home and tells me, "Oh, it was so beautiful," and I say, "This is great!" is it not a sign of how much he trusts me? Through this our relationship can grow. Trust deepens when we know that we can tell each other the truth.

Participating in the Global Love School means working together on solutions. With the background of this common global research, I can figure out how I personally want to live – be it as a monk, in a marriage, monogamously or with many love partners. No matter which way of life we choose, or which promises we give each other, it should protect our love and not deny the truth. As partners we can certainly choose to live monogamously. This choice can be very supportive on our common path. However, we should always re-member that we cannot own another human being. There is no legal claim to love.

The Path of Partnership

Is it possible for us to call something love that is not really love? Might it be possible that we always go back to the same painful ways because we are following information which has been false from the start?

It usually happens like this: When we first fall in love, we project everything beautiful onto our partner. He is the one and only, he will take care of me, he is my personal god, and vice versa, my personal goddess, my

Mary, my playmate who is there just for me. I adore her; she is my fulfillment forever.

But there is something at the core that we are not aware of. It is the historical pain in love that we have experienced once and never want to experience again. We have therefore buried it deep within us. We have erected defense mechanisms around it, and we defend ourselves and become aggressive and angry when someone or something approaches this place. If this irrational anger or fear has us in its grip, then the pain body is awakened.

We might have hoped to escape the pain body through our new love. Maybe we will be happy together for a while. For some weeks, perhaps for months, we will be able to play the role of the desired dream partner for the other.

But eventually something changes. No man or woman can permanently maintain the illusion of that which we project onto them. After a while, another face emerges, a face that we can hardly stand. All that we fear and find unbearable in the opposite gender rears its ugly head before our very eyes; and likewise, we wear this grotesque mask for our partner.

Now it is important to know that this other face is not the true self either. It is the face of the pain body. In an intimate relationship, sooner or later, the two genders meet, pain body to pain body. This is where all the suffering begins and it often ends in disaster.

There will be situations where we allow ourselves to be controlled by unconscious processes against our better judgement. In hindsight we feel ashamed and apologize a thousand times, and still we are driven to do the same thing again in the next situation. This is the permanent war in love. It is not about guilt here. Nobody can be declared guilty of unconscious processes. This is about realization. We should be grateful for every war that we have recognized in ourselves, instead of being ashamed of it, because once we have recognized something we can begin to accept responsibility and direct the process ourselves.

True partnership leads us through the hell of our pain body. If we discover what love really is we can go through and find a higher level of faithfulness. Then the path of partnership will be a path of enlightenment.

We then come to the question of how we find a form of faithfulness to each other where we do not have to hide our love or desire for someone else? How would it look... this way of living together in which the affection of one person for another does not trigger this level of fear, anger or jealousy in a third? How can a community support couples so that love endures?

If we really see the image of an intact community, we nurture healing information that goes far beyond us.

Biological Truth: The Logic of Sexual Attraction

The link between love and sexuality in our society often leads to misunderstandings. Existing society says the two should always go together. If I love somebody the most it means that I most desire him or her sexually.

This is usually true at the beginning of a love relationship because there is often great passion. But if it changes after a while it is perceived as a disaster, so long as we have not really thought through the question, *what is the logic of love, and what is the logic of sexual attraction?*

It was normal in ancient tribal cultures to develop a relationship, to have children together, to remain fully faithful to each other for a lifetime and, at the same time, to experience sexuality with others. Sexuality itself was sacred; it was a form of worship, a celebration, and not bound to relationships.

Once again, it is essential to find a whole picture of living together in which we no longer have to hide our biological truth.

I like to compare the healing of water with the healing of love and sexuality. Wilhelm Reich said, "It is not the river that overflows its banks which is violent, but the walls that have locked it in too narrow a bed." So it is with love and sexuality. If we lock them in too tight a vessel, they cannot develop in a healing way. The attempt to suppress sexual attraction cannot succeed. Its suppression causes its force to become destructive and violent. These elemental forces have the desire to flow freely, just like water. In this freedom we find the ethical orientation which supports our partnership.

Overcoming the Historical Trauma:
Working on a Minefield of Gender Relations

Since the project's inception in 1978, we have been conducting research into the subject of peace work in love. Today, after 35 years, we still cannot say that we have the solution and are free from all heartache and every sexual anxiety, but we are working on it, and a viable basis of solidarity among the people in Tamera has arisen for this purpose.

Sometimes guests and visitors are surprised that it is taking so long, but they should know that anybody doing research in the area of love and sexuality is working on a historical topic. We come from a long history of patriarchal violence. We are dealing with thousands of years of pain. The inquisition is not so far behind us. Building real trust between men and women is healing work for the collective pain body.

We can dare to delve to these depths in the Global Love School. We are working on the vision of a new society of partnership, where the male and the female parts are in equilibrium and where real trust is created between the genders.

I feel very happy. I have been living in community since 1978. My children grew up in community. For more than 30 years I have lived in a partnership in which we have set ourselves apart from jealousy, and where it has no power. My partner can go with any woman he wants to go with. I can meet other men. I can say that I lead a fulfilled life. I am very proud on one level.

On the other hand, we are still on a path of discovery. Like all couples who walk the long and deep path of truth, we touch a level where there are still things left unspoken. There are still areas where the unconscious reigns, in which anger and fear suddenly dominate. Where does this come from?

We call this level the minefield, an area where a careless remark can trigger an unexpected, violent emotion in the other. In living together, one learns to know and avoid the minefields of the other. Certain topics become taboo in order to avoid emotional explosions.

The minefields are the traumatic knot between the genders. These are the results of historical violations that women and men have inflicted upon one another. Wherever they did not find each other, wherever they could not land together with their love and desire, violence and destruction occurred, pain was inflicted, and retreat, hatred, anger, fear and bitter struggle were triggered.

It was so bad that we never wanted to touch this place again. We protected it and built an entire civilization of pretense around it. But couples that follow a long path together touch these knots again. Conflicts are inevitable. Most couples try to resolve their disputes in private. They bravely try to solve something without realizing that it is the social conditions of our culture that make a solution so difficult. From there they either agree to separate or they agree on a superficial coexistence where they no longer touch the hot spots. They therefore no longer touch their soul, their truthful core, and love is lost. One secretly looks around for other opportunities.

We want to dissolve this knot in the world, in ourselves and in our personal love relationships. And this is work.

War is mainly driven by our unconscious patterns, from the repressed parts of us. Healing work is consciousness work. Where there is consciousness, there can be no war.

The Love School is challenged with developing methods through which we can be witnesses to our hidden feelings and through which we find a language for them and make them ever more visible and easy to understand, in and amongst ourselves.

Let us take a look in the Global Love School at the issues that are not yet solved. The world needs places where research on love and sexuality can happen at this depth. Tamera works on answers in the environmental and technological areas, as well as for love, for evolution and revolution in Eros, for transformation and healing in love.

I am very grateful to the young generation that has studied in Tamera and made, on a very deep level, a decision to establish the Terra Nova School. For me, it is a necessary step to build an education platform where people all over the world study the same subjects, where they deepen their questions and exchange with each other so that they can see the questions, answers and solutions more clearly. I give thanks for the Terra Nova School. The Global Love School is a part of this education.

The Polarity of the Genders

Man and woman are the two halves of humanity. They are polar forces. How can we build their polarity so that a positive tension arises between them? What brings the genders into balance? This is a core research question of the Global Love School. We therefore ask the question anew: 'What does it mean to be a woman and what does it mean to be a man? What skills, opportunities, and tasks are associated?'

The emancipation of women was a historic first step of liberation, but it was also very painful, especially for the women themselves because the values of the women's movement developed in a societal environment that was still engraved with patriarchy. The demand for equality led to comparison with men. Many women wore themselves down under these standards. What is the true nature of the feminine identity? This is a research question that could not be so quickly answered.

The emancipation of women that we need today is not directed against men, and it does not go against our love for men, but it chooses to leave behind those male structures that have led to so much destruction on the planet.

The future that we seek is neither patriarchal nor matriarchal. It is a culture of partnership and trust between equally strong poles, man and woman.

This goes into the realm of religion and spirituality. The Divine is both feminine **and** masculine. In all ancient cultures, there was the Great Goddess, and there were gods and goddesses who were striving for a balance. That which is the same in all men and that which is the same in all women was worshiped in them. But the scale has tipped. Somewhat pointedly, we might say, 'You have robbed God of the goddess. It must have become pretty lonely in heaven. No wonder he has become so intolerant and punitive.' The pantheon of the future needs to bring back a place for the feminine so that there is peace on Earth.

We are living in a time of transformation. We are witnessing the birth of a new age. I hope that together we can find the orientation and visions to connect our work in crisis areas, with our local community building and with our inner peacework in love.

I wish us all a joyful, strong and deep time.

THE HEALING OF LOVE
Why the Issue of the Love Between the Genders had to Become the Central Focus of Our Project

Dieter Duhm, 2013

I am the founder of a community project now called Tamera. Tamera is a Peace Research Center in southern Portugal. The project has received worldwide recognition for its concepts of ecological and social renewal as well as for its global school, the "Global Campus," which disseminates the ideas of a new Earth. Since the beginning of our project, the focus of our research work has been the themes of sexuality, love and partnership. A humane culture emerges from the humane relationship between the genders. For this work, we founded the "Global Love School" under the leadership of Sabine Lichtenfels. I will explain below why we had to put the subjects of sexuality and love in the heart of our work.

On the news there was another one of these terrible stories from everyday life in Germany. While his wife was away, a normally inconspicuous, friendly man kills his three young children and then himself.

An isolated case? And the many similar cases? The daily drama of unsuccessful love relationships and marriages, the desperation of love partners, the suffering of children, and the ever increasing cycles of rage, and then the inevitable explosion: vengeance, violence and war. The themes of failed love, separation anxiety, jealousy and despair are not just a private matter, but a universal human issue. The drama of humanity is in large part the drama of unrequited love. How many murders must be attributed to unrequited love? How many women are beaten to death because men do not feel accepted by them? How much of the sorrow of children, how much disconsolate desolation is created anew every day in a society that has not solved its issue of love and its issue of sexuality? Once we have opened our eyes to the sorrow of the world there is no easy consolation, yet still global healing is possible.

The spiritual epicenter of the human world is the relationship of the two genders, of man and woman; because man and woman are the two halves of humanity they are spiritually and corporeally reliant on each other. Man and woman come together to create children. This act of procreation is intimately linked with a high physical and mental pleasure. What a gift from the universe that the propagation of the human race is connected with pleasure and joy! These two halves have to properly come together to insure that human life can proceed smoothly. There will be disasters if they do not merge properly – catastrophes such as cancer, child pornography, sadism, hatred, violence and war. The animal world also suffers because of the pain of man. The daily massacres that are committed against animals in slaughterhouses and laboratories are only possible because people have closed their hearts.

The unfathomable violence that is perpetrated against humans and animals all over the world today is the act of a closed heart. It is also an act of the banks, secret societies and multinationals, but their plans can only be implemented by a society that suffers from a collective closed heart. As long as the two halves of humanity do not come together properly there will be a calamity in our souls that cannot be healed by wealth and creature comforts. It is this calamity of unrequited love which, despite all moral or religious appeals, continues to repeatedly produce "evil." There are incredible things taking place behind the scenes of the bourgeois world. Marital rape, child abuse, family tragedies and murders out of jealousy are rampant. How it must look in an adult human's soul if they have to satisfy their sexual urges through sex with children! Moral outrage is no help here; the only help is the construction of a new sexual culture that returns the joy that man has lost in a world hostile to love.

The mystery of love and sexuality lies in the relation between the genders. The deepest human longing is for love, for spiritual as well as sensual, physical love. What bliss there is when a man and woman embrace for the first time – and yet, what of it remains after ten years? A fulfilled sexual life, like a fulfilled religious life, is a foundation of human happiness. The genders have sought and missed one another for centuries. They will continue to search and miss one another until a solution is found. The world is languishing in lovers' grief. The healing of this grief is a major global challenge of our time. We are facing a new stage of evolution. If the latent gender war ends, there will be no more war on Earth.

The global pain in love is the result of a several thousand year long history of war. It is the result of a chain of unimaginable atrocities that were committed against people, mainly women, in the name of patriarchal power. We all carry this collective trauma in our hereditary cellular memory. We all follow the unconscious information of fear and violence. In order to build the power of the church and state, the patriarchal world needed the repression of sexuality and subjugation of women under the command of male domination. The obedience of women was a condition of male potency. Sex and power were inseparably intertwined. Women who did not obey were punished or eliminated like Hypatia of Alexandria. In many countries unimaginable male violence against women took form. In the Middle Ages, in the year 1487, "Hammer of Witches" was published, a book about the execution of all women who were not needed for reproduction. The book was written by two monks and soon became the most widely read book in Germany after the Bible. One must hear this a few times before it can be believed. Consequently, women who stood out either by their attractiveness or by their will and courage were slandered as witches and burned alive. Burned alive!

Once one has perceived the global suffering of the female half of humanity, one wonders how there could still be women capable of love. This is a crucial point; and here I would like to thank the entire female gender. The female half of humanity must possess a very stable and faithful heart, faithful to the male half which abused and suppressed it for so many thousands of years. What madness! Humanity has blocked it's inborn joy, and thereby destroyed itself. Generation after generation, century after century, it has passed on the false propaganda that demonized the flesh and led to the chastisement of children and the burning of witches. What was originally intended to create joy and love was outlawed and persecuted. Thus humanity began to hate the things they once loved. Even today, our culture suffers for this perversion of values. The original sin of man is not carnality, but its suppression. The lust of the flesh was called "fornication" and cruelly eradicated. Since then, no truth has been possible.

The sexual nature of women is a gift from God as a dowry for a joyful life on Earth. The lust of the flesh is the deepest lust that has been given to us for the conscious understanding of life. But what woman can freely profess her nature, her desire and her sexual hunger? And what man may dare to speak of the "sexual nature" of women without being slandered as "sexist"? In every woman lives a part of that wild nature, which was intended to be tamed by marriage. And every man has also met Lilith in women and has felt fear before that sexual power. This wild nature fits neither into the housing of matrimony, nor into conventional notions of morality and decency. The plump wife, who lives obediently at her husband's side, is caught in a secret masquerade of constant lies. The man senses this, observes her and makes daily accusations. The children who receive too little love in such conditions, begin to lie, steal and get into fights – a tragic chain without end. We need a different ethic and a different sexual culture to be equal to the onslaught of sexual images and energies. When we think further, we need a new relationship to truth, to life and to all creatures; we need a new civilization initiated by the concept of global Healing Biotopes.

The center of our healing work is a new relationship between the genders. It is based on trust and solidarity. For the genders to be revealed to each other they need primal trust, which could hardly arise in the patriarchal era. We need a new way of interacting socially, new social structures and new pictures of love, so that the old despair can be overcome. We can liberate the world from war, if we are able to end the war in love. We can liberate the Earth from violence if we are able to end violence in sexuality – without suppressing our own wild nature! The passion is allowed to stay. If it is associated with trust it does not lead to violence, but to spirited tenderness. This is arranged beautifully in the plan of creation.

There is something inside of life that we all love endlessly. If humanity succeeds in giving continuity to this "something," we will have accessed a historic path of bliss. The wisdom of the East has created a beautiful aphorism, "The Tao is the way that cannot be abandoned. The way that can be abandoned is not the Tao." How about replacing the word "Tao" with this ever most deep, knowing love? And this is also always meant physically; knowing love goes through the body and through the flesh because "the word became flesh and dwelt among us." It is almost incredible how many truths we find in the Bible, if we look beyond the distortions and misrepresentations. The high point is found in the story of 'The Fall' when Adam ate the apple from the tree of knowledge and then discovered sexual pleasure. "And Adam knew his wife." In Hebrew they have the same word for knowledge and intercourse! They knew it!

The healing of love hardly happens at all in face-to-face meetings between partners, because they are too involved in their problem. This healing is a process of being born anew. To become capable of love we must learn not to become wrapped up in ourselves, but to participate in the world. Participation is part of the secret of love. This brings us inevitably into the field of ethics. Participation means trust, resolution of fear barriers, overcoming prejudices, and releasing the bolts with which we have locked our hearts. To become capable of love we must develop a system of life in which real trust between people arises and grows. The new centers, which we call Healing Biotopes, are greenhouses of trust. This is the crucial point. In order to free our communities from sexual falsehoods we have developed the concept of "free sexuality." But free love and free sexuality only make sense amongst people who trust each other. It is this trust that opens the heart and the body, dissolves the body armor and heals the soul. In Tamera we work on environmental and technological issues of healing water, permaculture and green energy, but the most important work is the creation of trust amongst the students, staff and children.

We need a functioning community in order to do these things. The issues that are connected with the area of sex, love and relationships, are much too heavy to be carried by two people alone. They are historical topics for all of humanity. We need communities that know these subjects and have agreed on a fundamental, absolute solidarity with all those who reveal their inner self as they share their issues. For this we have adopted the method called the SD Forum. SD means self-expression ("SelbstDarstellung"). It is a process in which the performer can unreservedly show himself, with his fears and conflicts, to the group without the threat of condemnation. This process is about learning true solidarity. When people recognize each other in their shared afflictions they feel less need to disguise themselves and can live together with greater trust. "To be seen is to be loved." This is a true statement. But it takes courage to let oneself be seen. We had to develop many unusual methods to find the way of truth in the field of love. We are far from finished, but we may have crossed the half-way point on the "suspension bridge." It has been a long and sometimes tedious work. Those who come to Tamera looking for quick sex should rather look elsewhere.

Some basic guidelines have emerged for the co-existence of the genders which could be included in the ethical canon of the foundation of a new culture:

1 Love is the great heritage of humanity.
2 Trust between the genders is the basis of a future without war. Never lie to your love partner.
3 You can only be truthful if you are allowed to love others. Free love and the love of a couple are not mutually exclusive, but complementary.
4 Jealousy is not part of love.
5 Partnership cannot be given life by people making claims on each other, but only by mutual support.
6 Sadism and masochism are the result of humanity's historical mistreatment of sexuality. As a matter of principle, violence is not part of sexuality and love.
7 No sex with children.
8 Sexual actions may never be conducted against the will of any person.
9 There is no ownership in love. Relationship problems cannot be solved legally, but only by the help of a supportive community.
10 If you have a choice between love and something else, follow love.

Behavioral patterns have emerged in the relationship of women towards men which we might call "gentle feminism." Women begin to explore their feminine source, and thus establish their own sovereign power, which no longer depends on a relationship with a single man. This establishes a new historic anchor point for women in the holon of life and human society. In her book "Weiche Macht" ("Gentle Power," not yet available in English), Sabine Lichtenfels formulated the new relationship between men and women. She writes,

"Over 3,000 years of history have been imprinted by the dominance of men establishing a principle of hard power. The power within male-dominated societies lie in breaking resistances, which was expressed as conquests, religious warfare as well as in their methods of education and handling nature. By using these methods, modern man has maneuvered himself into a dead-end from which he cannot escape without female support. We do not intend to re-establish ancient matriarchal structures, nor do we want to dominate or patronize men. Feminine power is not targeted at men, nor is it targeted against our love for men – it simply, decisively leaves behind those male structures that have led to the worldwide extinction of life and love. Unless women take a public stand, nobody can escape this dead-end. It is up to us women to assume the political and sexual responsibility again, the responsibility that has been abandoned for so long. We invite all dedicated men to join our peace work."

The healing of love between the genders is not limited to the relationship between the genders. It also includes a new relationship to nature, cooperation with all creatures, the healing of water and a loving relationship with animals. We need a reintegration of our human world in the overall world of life in order to heal our primal pain of separation. It's ultimately about reconnecting with "Omega," the divine center of all things. To love is to approach each other center to center, wrote Teilhard de Chardin. The aim of our work is the new Earth, Terra Nova. As long as a single child is still starving, a single girl mutilated, a single woman raped, a single animal tortured or a single young man forced to go to war, this world is not in order. We will continue our work.

For the solidarity and love between the genders.
For all children of the Earth.
For a future without war.

III THE MATERIAL BASIS

THE SECRET OF WATER AS A BASIS FOR THE NEW EARTH

Healing the Water Cycle through the Creation of
Water Retention Landscapes

Free speech by Bernd Walter Mueller, edited in 2013

*"Water, energy and food are freely available for all
humankind when we no longer follow the laws of capital,
but rather the logic of nature."*
Dieter Duhm

I put this quote at the beginning of my speech because
I want to ask you to see this vision of a healed world
as often and vividly as you can. We must not get
accustomed to a state where something that is actually
self-evident appears to us as an unrealistic utopia. A
world in which all people have free access to sufficient
water, energy and food is completely feasible. More
than eighty years ago similar ideas were described by
the Austrian man Viktor Schauberger, a brilliant water
researcher, a pioneer and visionary of the highest level.
Even then he could foresee the global problems that we
face today and he showed how they can be solved. One
key point of the solution is the right treatment of water.
I would therefore like to address the issue of water in
this lecture.

Water is life – and where there is life there is also nutrition and energy.

The years 2010 to 2020 were declared by the United
Nations as the "Decade for Deserts and the Fight
Against Desertification." Progressive desertification
is currently one of the biggest global problems. More

than 40% of the global landmass today is classified as dryland. Also in Europe, for example here on the Iberian peninsula, the desertification process is dramatic. One third of the land area of Spain has already transformed into dryland. Most of these dry areas are located in the even poorer countries of our planet Earth. Billions of people today have no access to good, fresh water. Even though we still try to push it aside, we know that this is partly connected with our lifestyle in the industrialized countries, which daily, hourly, and minute to minute leads to a situation in other regions of the Earth where children fall sick and die because of bad water, where humans fight over the last remaining water and animals die of thirst. Water, which is essentially the source of life, is today the cause of war, power struggles, disease, and an incredible amount of suffering.

The Bolivian President, Evo Morales demanded in his 2008 "Ten Commandments to Save the Planet, Life and Humanity," that we deal with this global water crisis and declare access to water as a human right. I fully support this demand. I am holding this speech so that all people and all animals regain free access to good drinking water. For this, the ideas of Water Retention Landscapes and the Terra Nova School have been developed.

Desertification Resulting from Incorrect Water Management

We humans have the knowledge of how to transform deserts and semi-deserts back into living landscapes traversed by fresh spring water streams. In most cases desertification is not a natural phenomenon but the result of incorrect water management on a global scale. Deserts do not arise because of a lack of rain, but because humans treat water in the wrong way.

Our landscape in the Alentejo is considered an arid region, and yet there has been very heavy rain in the last week. The amount of rain that fell over a few days would have been enough to supply the population of the whole region with water for drinking and household use for one year. Instead it ran off unused and caused additional damage. The fertile soil washed away, the earth under the foundations of bridges was washed away, and many roads, villages and towns were flooded. People are now busy repairing the inflicted damage. This is laborious and costly, and with the next rain the same happens again, so they have no time to think about investing in new systems that would ensure clean water year round and at the same time prevent floods.

We have a lot of rain in the Portuguese winter; and in summer it is dry. Only a few decades ago southern Portugal was a region where the streams flowed with water all year round, even during summer. Today the streams swell only during the rainy season and afterward they become dry again. The system has fallen completely out of balance. A similar situation can be found in all climate zones worldwide. Almost everywhere we can see widespread flooding and landslides with catastrophic consequences for humans, infrastructure, animals and nature. People then speak of natural disasters, but in reality they are man-made disasters.

The Half Water Cycle
How can we change this situation locally and globally? What does "system change" mean in the case of water management and how can we initiate it? To

find answers for this we have to look again at the actual situation we nowadays find everywhere. It corresponds to the half water cycle as described by Viktor Schauberger. Water evaporates, forms clouds and precipitates; the rain strikes the ground which can no longer absorb the water. Previously the globe was protected by a dense and diverse vegetation. Thus valuable humus could form, absorbing the water like a sponge.

Today, however, this diverse vegetation was largely destroyed, forests were cut, grasslands misused via over- or under-grazing, huge areas were "sealed" through urban development or unilateral use. The now unprotected ground warms up, but if the earth has a higher temperature than the rainwater it cannot absorb the rain, it closes itself, becomes hard, and the water runs off. It accumulates in large streams which flow away quickly. It strips away any remaining layer of topsoil, thus leading to the fatal problem of erosion. The fast-flowing water quickly fills streams and rivers. In heavy rain they swell up and carry a lot of soil and other material with them, but they cannot deposit this at the next bend in the river because the water is no longer allowed to meander, as the rivers have been straightened and their banks additionally reinforced. The precious soil that is so urgently needed on the land now causes the rivers to silt-up downstream. They become shallow and breach their banks, leading to great damage especially in the cities lying at the river mouths.

In the half water cycle we have rivers that no longer flow with clear spring water but with muddy polluted rainwater. There are no places where the water has time to gather itself, to rest, to mature, and to enrich itself with minerals and information. Hardly any young people on this Earth still know streams that carry clear spring water.

The Falling Water Table

If the water cannot sink into the body of the earth, then it is lacking in the aquifers. Through the resulting aridness, the soil life suffers, the micro-organisms retreat, the fertility of the land decreases significantly, and fewer and fewer plant and animal species can survive. Dry soil and the loss of biodiversity are the most important indicators of desertification.

The water table is falling – worldwide and dramatically so. The global supply of drinking water is diminishing. Here we face facts which directly lead us to apocalyptic scenarios if we do not manage to halt this process. Through the diminishing water table, the balance between the sweet groundwater and the salt water of the sea can no longer be maintained. The salt water invades inland unhindered, soils and deeper freshwater reservoirs become salinated. The ecosystem collapses – an almost irreversible situation. In many coastal areas worldwide this process is already happening. Also here on the Iberian Peninsula, the ground water begins to be salinated near the coastline.

But what kind of times does humanity approach if there is no more natural drinking water? Here we cannot turn away and allow something preventable to happen. The knowledge for preventing this catastrophe is available; now it is about applying it.

We know this is not how planet Earth is meant to be. This is not how the coexistence of humans, animals and Earth is meant to be. This is not how life is meant to be.

The Full Water Cycle

Let us look again at the healthy picture – it is the picture of the full water cycle. The rain which falls on the earth, will then be absorbed by a layer of humus. Not long ago on Tamera's land there was a living fertile soil layer of up to half a meter in depth. It was more or less like this throughout the whole of Portugal and in principle across all of Europe. This humus soil layer, which was shaded and rooted by plants, soaked up the rainwater, giving the water time to seep into the deeper ground layers and fill the body of the earth. In this way, a saturated earth-body acted as a storage organ. The water rests at different depths underground, sometimes over long periods of time. We still know little about what really happens to the water down there in the darkness. I feel this as the 'female' or 'soul' part of the water cycle. What we can say is that the water matures there by mineralizing itself and taking in information. This ability to take in and store information is one of the essential and most mysterious qualities of water.

In the saturated soil, the water cools down on its way through the deeper layers of the earth. Where the full water cycle is intact, the water returns to the surface as matured spring water with a temperature of +4°C. Such spring water has an immense healing power for the earth and all its creatures. Streams and rivers flowing with spring water have healing power for the land when they are allowed to meander in accordance with their true nature. The water increasingly vitalizes itself over the course of its flow. Life unfolds in diverse habitats on the banks of such streams and rivers.

The water in the full water cycle is flowing continuously and steadily. The earth acts as a buffer, as it can absorb a large amount of water at once but only slowly releases it. In this way floods are prevented, and at the same time the streams carry clear, clean water all year long.

The balance is reached between the rainy months and the dry seasons. In principle this applies throughout all climate zones. A full water cycle, in which the body of the earth completely fulfills its function, once again creates stability and equilibrium everywhere.

Healing Nature through Water Retention Landscapes

Today the humus topsoil of the earth has disappeared from a large percentage of the the surface of the planet. The erosion process, especially over the last decade, has progressed so rapidly and extensively that one can speak of it as a global disaster. This is why we must not delay ourselves by developing ecosystems which create a thin layer of humus after only thirty, forty or even more years. We need this balancing sponge-effect sooner. In order to complete the water cycle again we needed to find a way in which the water could be absorbed by the earth despite the missing topsoil layer. This is how the idea of Water Retention Landscapes developed.

Water Retention Landscapes are systems for the restoration of the full water cycle by retaining the water in the areas where it falls as rain. There are plenty of ways to hold the rainwater on the land that can be used in various combinations. For example with the creation of retention areas, "check dams," "swales," terraces, deep plowing along the "keylines" or by land stewardship such as reforestation, organic farming and special pasture management (eg. Holistic Planned Grazing).

The aim of this work is that no rain or waste water will runoff the area anymore. Then we have transformed a landscape into a "retention landscape." All outflowing water should be spring water. In Tamera we have created a series of interconnected retention areas (from pond-sized to lake-sized) in which the rainwater can collect behind a dam constructed from natural material. The retention spaces themselves are not sealed with concrete or any artificial membrane, so that the water can slowly but steadily diffuse into the body of the earth.

The term 'Water Retention Landscape' is always connected with the concept of nature-healing. The construction of Water Retention Landscapes is an active and effective answer to the destruction of nature.

This answer was developed in Tamera in deep cooperation with the Permaculture specialist Sepp Holzer of Austria and various visionaries and ecologists from around the world.

There are no regions of human habitation unsuitable for the construction of Water Retention Landscapes. Wherever ecosystems have been destroyed or degraded Water Retention Landscapes can, and should be, created – on every type of land, in every climate zone, on every hillside, and especially in areas with low precipitation, as here they are particularly important. The less precipitation that falls in an area, and the greater the length of time between rainy periods, the more urgent the development of a Water Retention Landscape becomes. But also in tropical high-rainfall regions Water Retention Landscapes will be a great step towards healing. The retention areas act in place of the fragile humus layer, which is sometimes completely washed away during only one rainy season after the clearance of the rainforests. Through their high water absorbing capacity, they also help to prevent fatal landslides which nowadays are caused more and more often by heavy rainfall. Thus they also directly save human lives.

Perhaps there are still a few forested areas on Earth where it is not yet necessary to intervene because there is still enough humus. But unfortunately today, these are rare cases. Water Retention Landscapes are the healing impulse urgently required by the earth and all her creatures. They can and must arise in every place where people regain the courage, strength and also of course, the knowledge needed to create them.

For this we now need a common and determined power and direction. In order to create Water Retention Landscapes worldwide, special education centers are required.

We have launched the Terra Nova School to disseminate the information via the Internet and support groups and initiatives to apply this knowledge in their own countries. In our vision, so-called model universities could develop anywhere through self-organization, where the theory and practice of retention landscape building can be learned.

In this way, a process of change is initiated that evidently includes all other aspects of human life. A Water Retention Landscape is sustainable only if the individual and social life is re-embedded into nature and the higher orders of creation.

How such an embeddment functions in modern times, and which technological and social knowledge is needed for it, should be researched and taught in the models and be available for all people who seek this knowledge.

The change-in-thinking process will ultimately only be completed when there is no longer a single living being on Earth lacking in water, nutrition and human compassion.

Getting to Know the Being of Water
The first step in the change of thinking begins with a new perception of water itself. A water retention space is not only to be understood technically but also exists in order to give an understanding of the being of water to new kinds of engineers. A water retention space has to be shaped in a way that the water does not stagnate, but on the contrary is able to move according to its being.

Water is not only a physical or chemical substance that the human may deal with at his convenience or merely according to industrial norms. Water is a living being. We modern people have to learn to understand this all over again. The shaping of the water retention spaces is therefore not arbitrary.

We observe water. How does it want to move? Which shapes of banks does it like? Which temperature and which differences in temperature does it like? Does it like to form waves or not?

All of these aspects are incorporated into our work.

As with every living being, water also needs to be allowed the freedom to move in accordance with its being. Water wants to roll, swirl, curve and meander – then it remains vital and fresh. By such movement it purifies itself; at the same time it also calms down and has time to seep into the body of the earth.

There are three important principles for the shaping of such water retention spaces:
• The longer side of the retention space is, if possible, laid out in the same direction as that of the prevailing wind. The wind then blows over a long surface, thereby

forming waves which oxygenate the water; oxygen is an important element for the purification of water. Wind and waves carry particles of debris to the shores where they are trapped by aquatic plants and eventually absorbed by them.

• Banks are never artificially straightened or reinforced, but created in meandering forms with both steep and gently sloping parts so that the water can roll and swirl. At least one part of the shore is planted with aquatic and waterside plants.

• Deep and shallow zones are created. In this way different temperature zones emerge, providing healthy thermodynamics in the water. Shaded shore areas support this process. Thus the diversity of aquatic organisms finds its suitable habitats.

The dam of a water retention space consists entirely of natural material: no artificial film or concrete is used. The vertical sealing layer of the dam consists of as fine a material as available, ideally clay, for which optimally the material excavated from the deep zones is used. It is connected to a watertight layer of subsoil that sometimes lies a few meters below the surface. The sealing layer is compacted and built up layer by layer with fine, earth-moist material. Then it is piled up from both sides with mixed earth-material, covered with humus or topsoil, and can then be landscaped and planted on.

Through this natural construction method, the water retention spaces fit in with the landscape and do not become incongruous with their surroundings. Life reappears on the shores after only a short time Finally the plants, especially the trees, are once again provided with water from below as is appropriate to their nature.

We can reduce artificial irrigation and eventually completely abstain from it.

The Helping Forces

In the construction of Water Retention Landscapes there is an abundance of helping forces from the kingdom of nature that stand by our side. Knowing this, the new engineers get in contact with these forces and ask them for their cooperation. There are millions upon millions of micro-organisms that immediately start their work the moment they notice that there is water, even after the rainy season. They are our best co-workers.

Most of them live invisibly in the earth. These beings sense that a sustainable healing process has been initiated here from which everything benefits. We might not see their effectiveness for a long time, but we know that they exist and quickly start their work. Eike Braunroth, an expert in the area of cooperation with nature, impressively describes in his book "In Harmonie mit den Naturwesen" ("In Harmony with the Beings of Nature") what happens when animals, previously considered as pests or vermin and fought against correspondingly, are finally recognized as cooperation partners. He writes about the example of slugs, aphids, voles, potato beetles and ticks.

"Their plentiful occurrence, their rampant reproduction, their unstoppable eating orgies in my garden, their resistance against my tricks opened my senses to a different consciousness of life... Today they all live an unimpeded existence. They showed me what nature is capable of: unconditional friendship."

In our ecological work in Tamera this aspect of cooperation is strongly incorporated. Birds for example, are necessary co-workers for afforestation because some seeds need to pass through a bird's stomach in order to germinate. Here lies a fascinating area of work and research.

There are also helping forces still quite unfamiliar to us. Through Dhyani Ywahoo, a Cherokee spiritual teacher, we learned that lightning is an important factor in the revitalization of weakened soil if it is again moist enough. In her book, *Voices of Our Ancestors: Cherokee Teachings from the Wisdom Fire,* she writes,

"As those aquifers are depleted, the electrical energy of lightning has no place to be called to. The lightning activity is the pulse, just as the nervous system is the pulse that animates your body. So, as these aquifers are further depleted, there is less and less energy for growth, for life. There are also more subtle effects of the lightning."

Sepp Holzer has discovered that thunder is also a helping force for the growth of various species of edible mushrooms.

With these examples we see how much exciting research work still lies in front of us.

With the establishment of Water Retention Landscapes humankind re-enters the cooperation with the spirit of the earth, and with the spirit of plants, animals and human beings that live, or are meant to live, in this space. In creating these systems it is not only about engineering but about the art of contact with the living and about the recognition that we humans are not the only beings living on this planet. Creation has been entrusted to us in order for us to perceive and care for it. This is the original role of humankind on Earth. Here the knowledge, which in former times all indigenous people possessed, is reawakened and transferred into modern life.

The Water Retention Landscape of Tamera

We began the construction of the first water retention space in 2007 in Tamera. The proposal for it came from Sepp Holzer, who has supported us for a long time in the renaturalization and healing of Tamera's land. Until then we thought we lived in a dry country. When he showed us the dimensions of the first planned water retention space the question arose of how long it would take for such a large basin to fill up with water. 'Lake 1,' as it is known today, is located in the center of our site. The idea of having to watch over a dusty, half-empty pool for years did not motivate us to take this first step towards the planned Water Retention Landscape. Then, to make things clear to ourselves, we had the idea of calculating the average annual amount of precipitation falling upon the catchment area of the retention space. In our minds we filled this water into containers, each with a capacity of one cubic meter, and placed them one after the other in a row that reached a length spanning the almost one thousand kilometers from Tamera to Barcelona. That was enough to launch us out of the system of scarcity thinking.

In the very same year we began with the construction. In the first winter the lake and the adjoining body of the earth filled up a good two-thirds with water. After the second rainy season, which had below average precipitation, only a few centimeters to the highest potential water level remained to be filled. In the third winter, so much rain fell that we could have filled several more retention spaces. Today, only four years after the construction began, it is as if there had never been anything other than a water retention space. Many people who visit Tamera for the first time cannot believe at first that it is anything other than a natural lake. On the terraces by the shore we have created an edible landscape and planted thousands of fruit trees and shrubs. Wild animals, such as the otter, have settled here.

And the birds have returned. We have observed 93 different species of birds in Tamera, some of which are very rare species found only in water-rich areas. Already within the first year a new seepage spring arose, which since then has flowed continuously throughout the year.

The construction of Lake 1 was only the beginning. Since then we have created a number of further water retention spaces.

In 2011 we built a retention area, which has about three times the capacity of Lake 1. With this construction we have made a breakthrough in the first valley from a landscape with plenty of water to a retention landscape. This area is now prepared to fully absorb even strong continuous rainfall.

This large retention area is located at the highest point of the valley. The water pressure will be high enough to irrigate all of the land (as long as this is still necessary), without having to supply additional energy for pumping. With the water from this highest-situated retention space the water level of the following retention spaces will remain almost stable all year round.

Here in Tamera we want to demonstrate a model of how it could look everywhere in the Alentejo and basically everywhere in the world. Without water there is no life. With water there is life. We are becoming ever more able to see and maintain the picture that is emerging in front of our eyes if we ask ourselves,

'How does it look if we live with water and not without water?'

How quickly we come to visions of paradise and how quickly we can step out of scarcity thinking on all levels! I would like to conclude with a quote from Viktor Schauberger. It comes from an essay he wrote in 1934 in the book, *Das Wesen des Wasser* ("The Being of Water").

"Everything originates from water. Therefore, water is the universal natural resource of every culture or the foundation of every physical or mental development. The unveiling of the secret of water will put an end to all manner of speculation or calculation and their excesses, to which belong war, hatred, envy, intolerance and discord of every kind. The thorough investigation of water therefore truly signifies the end of all monopolies, the end of all domination and the beginning of a socialism arising from the development of individualism in its most perfect form. If we succeed in unveiling the secret of water, in understanding how water can emerge, then it will become possible to produce all qualities of water in any location, and then one will be able to make vast areas of desert fertile; then the sale value of food and also that of machine power will fall so low that it will no longer be worthwhile to speculate with it."

I ask everyone to perceive this vision. I ask everyone to see how the human being is meant to be, to see the true standing of the human and the role creating models plays in this. A person who takes his human rights back into his own hands also takes a stand once again for the rights of water, as demanded by Evo Morales, and will enter into cooperation with nature and its beings. When we have found the inner picture of reconnection with nature again then we begin to understand the sentence,

"Water, energy and food are freely available for all humankind, when we no longer follow the laws of capital, but rather the logic of nature."

This is how life is meant to be.
Thank you for listening.

PEACE WITH NATURE AND ALL FELLOW CREATURES

Excerpt from the Book: The Sacred Matrix

Dieter Duhm, 2001

*"As long as humans torment, torture and kill animals,
we will have war."*
Bernard Shaw

Sunday morning. Today I am in the bathtub and I
notice some tiny insects on the tiles of the wall. They are
very thin and maybe 3 millimeters long; they have many
legs. I decide to regard them as ants. Where do they
come from? What do they eat? What are they doing on
this wall?

I become curious, for they are my fellow creatures in
evolution, they are real living beings, and they are part
of the one existence, so they must be cosmically related
to me in some way. I watch them on their Sunday walk
on the vertical wall and I see how they disappear into
a little hole. That is their apartment. They have actually
built themselves an apartment in the plaster between
the tiles. What occurred in them as they did this?
Where did they get the enthusiasm and the power to be
able to do something like that? Normally one sees them
as pests and cleans them off.

Two worlds collide with each other here, and one of
them, the older one, has to give way. This may be fully
in line with Darwin, but is it also right in a higher
sense? Do we humans really have the right to destroy
an element of life as if this were natural just because
it doesn't fit into our own system of life? Is the ants'
system of life wrong – or is ours? Maybe our own system of life is not quite correctly adapted to the higher

order of creation? Is there a possibility for non-violent coexistence?

Just a few decades ago such thinking would have been characterized as absurd, but today it becomes increasingly relevant with every further consideration, and with every new experience. Maybe there is a possibility for a kind of coexistence that encompasses all living beings? We will see.

Chaos research has taught me one thing: things that collide on the existing level of order can harmonize at a higher level of order. If enmities arise within a certain system, they can transform into friendship at the level of a system of a higher order. The solution of many issues consists in finding a higher level of order.

The global agrarian production of food is connected to chemical warfare that human beings are waging against "pests." These are innumerable small living beings that inhabit every field and every garden, and naturally want to partake in the harvest. There are, for example, worms, caterpillars, snails, aphids, mice, moles, etc. Chemical warfare is not aligned with the Sacred Matrix, for here the human being is destroying other organs that belong to the whole just as we do. There is an alternative which has proven itself effective in small model projects.

There are non-violent gardens on Earth. They are described in the book "In Harmonie mit den Natur-wesen" ("In Harmony with the Beings of Nature") by Eike Braunroth. The principle is based on communication with the so-called pests, not on their destruction. The peace gardeners use neither pesticides nor any other methods of deterrent against the small creatures. Peace is established through an agreement between human beings and their fellow creatures.

Jürgen Paulick, for example, a student of Eike Braunroth and, until his death, a co-worker at Tamera, made the following agreement:

"I have planted a bed of lettuce; it belongs to all of us. I will harvest twelve heads of lettuce and you can have three."

Sometimes he put down such agreements in writing on a piece of paper that he then placed in the garden. I can imagine a nice heading in a tabloid newspaper: "Alternative Gardener Writes Letter to Pests." At first we may react similarly and shake our heads. The thing is that it works.

We in Tamera have had contact with animals in a way that one would not have believed possible if one had not experienced it. It is based on the fact that all animals and human beings are parts of the one existence and of the one consciousness. The information must be unambiguous and consistent. It must come from an authentic spirit of peace, not from reluctant concessions. In the surroundings there must be no signs of violence or destruction, also not in the form of complicity products, for whose production animals had to be killed.

Do snails know the number three? Probably not, but neither do they have to know it. A computer also does not have to understand what one inputs, and yet it does the right thing because it was programed to do so by a higher authority. We have a similar situation with the snails and the other animals. If we formulate our request clearly enough, and if it makes sense, it will be taken up by the information pattern which controls the snails and will be transmitted to the snail as a behavioral impulse. The same is true for a spider that is building its web. Does the spider know how to construct a web? The meta-intelligence which oper-ates in the body of the spider through the spider's information grid, knows how, and in the circuitry of creation, this is enough.

In the case of the peace garden, horticulture is a spiritual process of information and cooperation, from beginning to end. Everything is one existence and one continuum: the garden soil, the plants, the animals, the human being, and the world of the microbes are all parts of **one** life body. All subjects that participate in this life body are connected with each other through the right frequency in **one** information circuit.

IV APPENDIX

Dr. Dieter Duhm

Historian, author and psychoanalyst, Dieter Duhm was born in 1942 in Berlin and is the initiator of the "Healing Biotopes Plan," a global peace plan. Beginning in 1967 he engaged in the Marxist left, including being one of the leading characters in the students' movement. In 1972 his well-known book "Angst im Kapitalismus" (Fear in Capitalism) was published, which made the link between the thoughts behind political revolution and the liberation of the individual.

1975 saw a distancing from leftist dogmatism and a shift towards a more thorough human alternative, leading to the establishment of the 'Bauhütte' project: a three year social experiment with 40 participants in the Black Forest in Germany. With the theme of 'founding a community in our times' the experiment embraced the questions of the origin, meaning and aim of human existence on planet Earth. Arising from the experiment come outlines of a new possibility of existence with the concepts of 'free love,' 'spiritual ecology' and 'resonance technology.'

In 1995, along with theologian Sabine Lichtenfels and others, he founded Tamera Peace Research Center in Portugal, which today has more than 160 co-workers.

Dieter Duhm has dedicated his life to creating an effective forum for a global peace-initiative, which is a match for the destructive forces of capitalistic globalization.

Sabine Lichtenfels

Born 1954 in Münster, she is a theologian and peace activist. In the stone circle of Almendres, near Évora, in Portugal she experienced for the first time that she was able to come into contact with a primordial human knowledge by way of her mediumistic gifts. She discovered that, far beyond our reckoning of time, a peaceful tribal culture had existed, which cooperated with nature and had a high knowledge of love and of community life. They had a premonition of their own downfall and retained their knowledge of a harmonious life in tune with the Goddess in their stone circles. Sabine Lichtenfels named their universal and community-oriented way of life "pre-historic utopia." She took it as a role model for a community of the future and for a peace university, which she founded with Dieter Duhm and others in Southern Portugal: The Healing Biotope I Tamera. Sabine Lichtenfels wrote two books about her discoveries and the research in the stone circle: "Traumsteine" (Dream Stones) and "Tempel der Liebe" (Temple of Love).

In 2013 she founded the Global Love School to anchor and spread this pre-historic knowledge globally.

Bernd Walter Mueller

Born 1962 in Cologne, he is a nature researcher, specialist in the construction of Water Retention Landscapes, permaculturist. Since 2007, he is a co-worker of the Peace Research Center Tamera in Portugal, in close coopeation with Sepp Holzer. Today Bernd Mueller is the director of the Ecology Department of Tamera and a teacher in the Global Campus, an international training center for peace workers.

In 1986 he abandoned his engineering studies in the traditional university system because he did not find the answers he sought. He started his own business, ran a health food store, worked in landscape gardening and later in tree care.

In 1989 he emigrated to Spain and managed an organic farm in the Sierra Nevada. There he found the necessary calmness to study natural processes through intense observation. He discovered a new, more subtle possibility of cooperation between human beings and nature.

Today he transfers the insights from this process of self-education into the practical development of ecological models for landscape healing and the restoration of the earth.

Monika Alleweldt

Born in 1954 in Giessen, she has degree in Agricultural Engineering. An agricultural internship in Guatemala marked a turning point in her life. Deeply moved by her impressions of a nation in the Global South, where the civil war

is now escalating into a genocide of the indigenous population, she began searching for the key elements of an effective way to offer aid to the world. In 1986 she came across the "Bauhütte," a project initiated by Dieter Duhm, Sabine Lichtenfels and others, which was the forerunner of the Tamera Peace Research Center. It was here that she found compelling fundamental ideas for the changes she sought. Since that time, she has been engaged in the context of Tamera, especially in the areas of public relations and publications.

ABOUT THE EDITOR:

Martin Winiecki
Born in 1990. Since his early youth he has been politically engaged in his hometown of Dresden. From 2006 to 2009 he was a student in the peace education in Tamera, Portugal and has been a co-worker of the project ever since. Since 2009 he has been part of the Institute for Global Peace Work in Tamera, working for the implementation of a global network. Since May 2013 he has taken on the coordination of the Terra Nova School.

Further Information:
We invite everyone who loves these thoughts and wants to support their manifestation, to take part in the Terra Nova School.

Institute for Global Peacework • Tamera
Monte do Cerro • P 7630-392 Reliquias • Portugal
Ph. +351 283 635 484 • igp@tamera.org
www.tamera.org

Donations:
The Terra Nova School is supported by a team of young people working on a volunteer basis. The project relies on regular monthly donations, so that participation in the school can continue to be offered free of charge. The donations will be used for the lessons, including the development of videos and audio recordings as well as for translating them into different languages and distributing and delivering them online.
We are grateful for any contribution!

Name: G.R.A.C.E.
Bank: Caixa Crédito Agrícola S. Teotónio
Account Number / NIB: 004563324023830233193
IBAN: PT50004563324023830233193
BIC: CCCMPTPL
Keyword: Terra Nova School

It is possible to make donations via PayPal too, please contact us: igp@tamera.org.

Literature for Further Study:

Dieter Duhm: **The Sacred Matrix. From the Matrix of Violence to the Matrix of Life**

Dieter Duhm: **Towards a New Culture. From Refusal to Re-Creation***

Dieter Duhm: **Future Without War. Theory of Global Healing**

Dieter Duhm: **Eros Unredeemed**

Sabine Lichtenfels: **Temple of Love. A Journey into the Age of Sensual Fullfillment**

Sabine Lichtenfels: **GRACE. Pilgrimage for a Future Without War**

Sabine Lichtenfels: **Sources of Love and Peace. Morning Prayers**

Leila Dregger: **Tamera. A Model for the Future**

Madjana Geusen (ed.): **Man's Holy Grail Is Woman**

Teilhard de Chardin: **The Phenomenon of Man**

Riane Eisler: **The Chalice and the Blade: Our History, Our Future**

Sepp Holzer: **Desert or Paradise?**

Jacques Lusseyran: **And There Was Light**

Peace Pilgrim: **Her Life and Work in Her Own Words**

Wilhelm Reich: **Character Analysis**

Wilhelm Reich: **The Function of the Orgasm**

* This book is freely available at: www.towards-a-new-culture.org

Satprem: **On the Way to Supermanhood**

Viktor Schauberger: **Nature as Teacher: New Principles in the Working of Nature**

Michael Talbot: **The Holographic Universe**